ARE THORESEN

A doctor of vete... ..., ...e, he has also studied anthroposophic medicine, homeopathy, acupuncture, osteopathy and agriculture. Since 1981 he has run a private holistic practice in Sandefjord, Norway, for the healing of small animals and horses, as well as people. He has lectured widely, specializing in veterinary acupuncture, and has published dozens of scholarly articles. In 1984 he started to treat cancer patients, both human and animals, and this work has been the focus of much of his recent research. He is the author of *Demons and Healing* (2018), *Experiences from the Threshold and Beyond* (2019) *Spiritual Translocation*, *The Lucifer Deception* (both 2020) and *Transforming Demons* (2021) and several other books on complementary medicine published in various languages.

The fireplace of our living room opposite which I meditate

TRAVELS ON THE NORTHERN PATH OF INITIATION

Vidar and Balder, the Three Elemental Realms
and the Inner and Outer Etheric Worlds

Are Simeon Thoresen, DVM

TEMPLE LODGE

Dedicated to All Who Seek to Heal and Understand

Temple Lodge Publishing Ltd.
Hillside House, The Square
Forest Row, RH18 5ES

www.templelodge.com

Published in English by Temple Lodge in 2021

Originally self-published in a series of books entitled: *The Northern Way of Initiation, The Three Realms of the Elemental World, Beyond the Three Elemental Worlds* and *Vidar and the Outer Etheric Realm* via CreateSpace in 2020 and 2021. This edition has been compiled from the above books and heavily re-edited by Temple Lodge Publishing in cooperation with the author

This book has been made possible through the philosophical and editorial support of some good friends: Glenn Charles, Michael Allen, Andrew Linnell and Sevak Gulbekian. Thanks to them all. (The author)

© Are Simeon Thoresen, DVM 2021

A CIP catalogue record for this book is available from the British Library

ISBN 978 1 912230 83 9

Cover by Morgan Creative
Typeset by Symbiosys Technologies, Visakhapatnam, India
Printed and bound by 4Edge Ltd., Essex

'Here I shall give the name "elemental world" to the first world that the soul of a human being enters on becoming clairvoyant and crossing the threshold. Only a person who wants to carry the habits of the sense world into the higher supersensible worlds can demand a uniform choice of names for all the points of view the higher worlds can offer."*

– Rudolf Steiner

---

* From *Secrets of the Threshold*, GA 147, lecture 3.

Contents

Preface

Very early in my life I developed a certain kind of clairvoyance, so that sometimes I could observe spiritual beings, especially those connected to nature such as trees, plants, water and wind. This ability was achieved by 'merging' or 'fading' into nature and experiencing it in full consciousness, just as described in the *Kalevala*, in *Parsifal* and Rudolf Steiner's lectures in Helsinki.* However, I was always conscious, logical and able to think clearly during my venturing into the spiritual or elemental realms, so that my experiences were never atavistic.†

Through many years, I systematically developed this ability, so that, at the beginning of March 2020, I thought that this world of the 'etheric' and 'elemental' beings – described by myself and other clairvoyant writers – really was the 'totality' of the etheric/elemental world. I now know that it was only the 'inner' etheric world, together with the third elemental realm.

During the after-effects of Covid-19, which I contracted at the beginning of the coronavirus pandemic, I experienced a deep penetration into the elemental world, through three completely different areas or realms, and thus understood that I had previously only been observing a superficial aspect of the elemental world. On 'each side' of these elemental realms, I could observe two distinct areas of the etheric world: the inner, that I had been able to observe earlier, and an outer part, that was totally new to me.

*

Before going more deeply into these questions, I will describe briefly the method and technique that I developed and used in my early years to pass the – first and second – thresholds of the spiritual world. I will call this technique 'fading', a method that is equivalent to the Northern path, the Outer way or the Macrocosmic way of initiation. We will see and understand that this general technique

---

Spiritual Beings in the Heavenly Bodies and in the Kingdoms of Nature, SteinerBooks 2011.

†With the exception of an instance in Ireland, described in my book *Transforming Demons*, Clairview Books 2021.

can be used in several variations, and that these variations can be used for traversing the different kinds of thresholds, of which there are many.

Some thresholds are 'greater' and some are 'minor'. The thresholds between the material world and both the third realm of the elemental world and the inner etheric world are major thresholds (maybe because they are the first to be traversed), as is the threshold between the first realm of the elemental world and the outer etheric world. The others are, in my experience, minor thresholds.

I will describe the actual crossing of the thresholds using this 'fading' method. The fundamental technique, as I have used and developed it, is to define or separate one part of yourself from the rest and, with this part, to 'drift' into the surroundings. I will describe how a part of you can be separated from the rest. The passing of the threshold, the separation of a part of oneself, is often initiated by a certain 'shock'. In my early years, such shocks appeared by destiny or chance, but later, and today, I can induce such shocks myself.

*

My personal method of fading into the elemental world changed abruptly and fundamentally in 2020. In early March I was lecturing in Forest Row, England, and it was very likely that I became infected there with the coronavirus Covid-19. On returning home to Norway, I didn't feel that anything was wrong – I was completely fine. By the middle of March, Norway decided to quarantine all those that had been abroad, and my clinic was also closed by governmental decree. It was then that I got a fever, alternating with heart pain, headache, stomachache and bleeding from the nose, as well as visual disturbances for about eight days. Then it all was over… Or so I thought.

I tried to saw a plank of wood, but could not because I immediately became completely exhausted. After that, I could do no physical work for some two months; then, I slowly managed to do some physical activity, a little more each day, until by July I was back to around 70% of my usual strength. During this period of utmost weakness, deep exhaustion and feeling half dead, I didn't ever consider taking medication, contacting a doctor or calling the hospital. I usually accept and embrace illness, considering why this particular disease has come to me, how it works with my karma and how I can grow through accepting and embracing it.

Whilst still exhausted from Covid, one morning at 8 am, during my wife's and my regular morning meditation in front of our fireplace, my spiritual view suddenly changed – or, should I say, deepened. As mentioned, most of my life I have been able to 'see' at a certain level, deeper than the material world, into what I have described in several of my books as the 'etheric world' or level (although now I understand that it was actually a combination of the inner etheric world and the third realm of the elemental world). But now another, deeper, level suddenly appeared.

I was focusing on the Norwegian soapstone of our fireplace. This time, due to my total exhaustion, I sank, or faded out, into it without any resistance or pre-conception, but with just an observant mind or soul. What I then 'saw' was something totally new. I was amazed as I had never thought about this consciously, although I was aware that there were multiple and deeper layers in both the elemental, etheric, astral and spiritual worlds.

It was 'in' the stone of the fireplace that I now 'saw' one of these deeper layers for the first time. I perceived the elemental beings and forces that made up the stone itself at an *atomic level*. A few days later, an even deeper layer appeared – deeper than the atomic forces. It was like a 'void' of elemental forces, existing in vacuum, expressing both the danger of the Azuras, the blessings of the Archai and, with them, the first angelic hierarchy. It was an open portal to the whole cosmos.

Quite soon, I understood that these two new levels had to be the second and the first elemental realms. This opening of my spiritual eye was due to the total embracing and acceptance of my 'half dead' state for four months, following the infection by Covid-19.

I slowly recovered from the illness, gaining back most of my strength by the summer of 2020. Then in August, however, I had a relapse of the disease, and was transferred back into the former half-dead state I had experienced since March. Again, I sat in front of my fireplace in the morning, meditating, gazing into the soapstone, observing the three realms of the elemental world. This time I was able to go in further, to the border of the first realm. Suddenly, after pushing on the threshold, I traversed it, finding myself *beyond it*. I will describe some of my experiences in greater detail later in this book.

I became infected by Covid-19 (by the so-called 'Kent' or 'English' variant) for the second time around New Year 2021. This time, I was not changed markedly, as nothing repeats itself in the spiritual world.*

*

The method of crossing the threshold by experiencing a shock has followed me throughout my life. Any minor or major shock can push me over the threshold. Different shocks that have caused this include a sudden fear, watching happenings that seem to be impossible or unbelievable, keeping awake when wanting to sleep, facing situations that could lead to death, or similar 'jolting' experiences. In later years, I induced such a shock by, for a moment, stopping my breathing or my heart beating.

After this small initial shock, I let some part of my soul or physical body *die or go to sleep*. Then, I *enter with my 'I'* into this sleeping part, after which I let the 'dying' part 'flow out' (separate) in certain directions. The directions are quite important for where you may find yourself after the passing. (This is much like how it is described in the film *The Matrix*, where *how* you went through a door decided where you ended up.)

- Going out with my separated thoughts into the cosmos, in an upward direction, at an angle of 45° to the horizon, makes me enter a 'brighter and lighter' part of the elemental world.
- Going with my feelings, projecting them out into the wide expanses of the world, parallel with the horizon, makes me enter the emotional area of the elemental world.
- Going into other beings with my feelings, especially animals that are suffering, and co-experiencing their suffering, makes me enter the 'animalistic' part of the elemental world.

---

* Later, in the winter of 2021, I also attracted a 'normal' flu. This was an amazing experience, as I heard and watched the 'archaic' spirit of Covid-19, who still had a certain hold over me, arguing or conversing with the lower, possibly archangelic, spirit of the flu, about which one of them should be in charge. The result was that I escaped them both, at least for a while.

- Letting the will flow down into the earth, in a forward direction, at about 45°, makes me enter darker and demonic areas of the elemental world.

This distinction and choosing of the area where to enter the elemental world, and to cross the threshold in certain areas, demands an ability to differentiate between thinking, feeling and will.

The separation of thinking, feeling, will and time

To understand and describe the techniques of *separating*, I must first point to where the silver cord connecting and controlling the soul fragments is situated. The anchor-place of this cord is, for me, three-fold, just as the soul is threefold in thinking, feeling and will – with the fourth addition of 'time'.

- Regarding *thinking*, the silver cord is anchored in the brain. (And, in the area of the third eye, we can find the physical anchoring of the 'I'-function.)
- Regarding *feeling*, the silver cord is anchored in the four chambers of the heart. (Here in the heart, we can find the physical anchoring of the 'I'-function.)
- Regarding *will*, the silver cord is anchored in the warmth of the blood, streaming through the limbs. (And here, too, we can find the physical anchoring of the 'I' function.)

In Buddhist meditation, some monks report that they reach Nirvana more easily by cooling the blood of the limbs through sitting out in the cold, which clearly shows the difference between the pre-Christian method of passing the threshold and the post-Christian one, as Christ *is* the 'I', and the 'I' lives in the warmth of the blood. Nirvana is eternal bliss without the Christ, and I believe that today this method is dangerous.

So, when I travel into the spiritual world via my soul fragments, I keep the connection via the silver cord anchored in my brain, blood or in the heart's chambers.

Concerning the heart, I can be more specific. In the heart chambers we have, in my experience, four levels of 'I' consciousness: the lower 'I', the normal 'I', the higher 'I' and the Christ 'I', which I have found to be centred in the following chambers:

- The lower 'I' in the right front chamber.
- The normal 'I' in the right main chamber.

- The higher 'I' in the left front chamber.
- The Christ 'I' in the left main chamber.

Firstly, I have to be conscious of my will, feelings and thinking, and to be aware of the time aspect – in which year, day and life I am living. Then, I concentrate on one of these abilities and imagine it in front of me, after which I let it fade away into the distance. Usually, I choose the thinking or the feeling. If it is the thinking, I let it 'fade' or 'fly away' at an angle of about 45° in an upward direction, and if it is the feeling, I see it straight, parallel to the ground. Also, I imagine deliberately that this ability is still connected to my body by means of a thin silver chord that is not straight, but goes like a flowing current between the loosening soul-abilities and either the third eye (thinking), the heart (feeling) or the lower abdomen (will). After any one of these abilities are projected outwards, I always experience certain changes within myself.

Separating the thinking:
If *thinking* is projected out from the area of the third eye, my ability to think in an *intelligent* way is lessened. If I want to hold my intelligence, I need to pull my departed thinking back, but as long as the thinking stays outside, it is of no great *intellectual* value. However, some part of the thinking remains in the brain, as a connection to the projected part.

Thus, I experience two types of thinking on each side of the connecting silver cord. The thinking that remains in my brain is much simpler than the one that is projected outwards. It is a totally body-related intellectual thinking, while the thinking that is projected outwards is more like a living, flowing cosmic thinking. My contact with the expelled thinking is through the silver cord, so when this connection is open, cosmic thoughts can be experienced also in the remaining brain-bound thinking, my 'nucleus'. It is possible to follow the projected thinking through the silver cord and experience the excarnated thinking directly, in its full glory. If the cosmic thinking is experienced out in the cosmos without being experienced through the 'nucleus', the memory of this thinking wanes almost immediately, as explained earlier. When I observe cosmic thinking from the side of the 'nucleus', it is possible to remember much more and be conscious of the results of this thinking.

The effect of the cosmic part of thinking without going through the 'nucleus' is a strongly joyful and light-filled experience, but without memory. The effect of thinking via the 'nucleus' is a much calmer experience. It is as if the surroundings, the periphery, become a little darker – the landscape in front of me becomes a somewhat violet or purple colour and my vision gets a little tilted to the right, so I tend to hold my head some 15° to the right, in order to correlate with the tilted vision.

I thus have two options:

- I can stay in my body, just watching the thinking being outside via the 'nucleus'.
- I can go directly through the silver cord, into the translocated thinking.

If I choose the first option, I can watch the world from both inside the 'nucleus' and also from the cosmic part via the nucleus. The thoughts then become a mix of both cosmic and earthly thinking.

If I choose the second option, I can watch the world from inside the separated thinking, and then the clear thoughts re-appear, not as my own, but as cosmic thoughts. With this separated or faded thinking, I can watch hidden worlds, see through the earth and also see through flesh, an ability I often use to find old trauma in my patients. This description also fits the separation of the feeling (but not the will).

Separating the feeling
In *feeling*, the main outpouring, fading away or 'port' of separation is the heart. When the feeling is projected out from the heart towards the periphery, the feelings that are left as the 'nucleus' change in the same way as the thinking: they get dull and grey. The fragment that departs seems to contain the 'better part' of the feelings. These colourful feelings leave me, and as long as I stay or remain in the body, I experience only dull and grey feelings. These remaining feelings are of a calmer and quieter variety. It is as if the etheric counterpart of the feelings remains in the form of the nucleus I have been describing, and that the astral part has left.

Between the remaining and the expelled feelings, there is a silver cord. Through this cord, I can travel with the 'I' from the nucleus to the expelled part, and as such choose where I want to stay. If I stay in the nucleus, I stay outside the macrocosmos. If I transpose my 'I' consciousness through the silver cord into the transposed or separated feelings, I can use these outer feelings as a sense organ for the entire cosmos.

The effect of feeling in the cosmic part, without going through the 'nucleus', is a strong joyful and light-filled experience, but *without* memory. Feeling via the nucleus is a much calmer and also darker experience. It is as if the surroundings, the periphery, become a little colder. This feeling is *with* memory.

As in thinking, in feeling I also have two options:

- I can stay in my heart, feeling both inside the heart and/or in the cosmos, connected via the silver cord.
- I can go directly through the silver cord into the translocated feeling.

If I choose the first option, I can use my feeling heart as a sense organ, from both inside the nucleus and also from the cosmic part via the nucleus. Then the feeling observations are a blend of the cosmic-and-earthly feeling heart.

If I choose the last option, I can watch the world from inside the separated feeling, and then the bright and joyous aspect of feeling appears, not as my own, but as *cosmic* feeling. This cosmic feeling is much brighter and more colourful.

Separating the will

If my *will* is projected out from the lower abdomen towards the interior of the earth, I first feel this separation as a certain loss of will. I feel unable to do anything. As with the thinking and feeling, there is still a remaining nucleus of the will that I can operate autonomously. In will, the experience of both the excarnated fragment and the remaining nucleus is somewhat different from both thinking and feeling. The main difference is that I have difficulties in observing both the material world and the spiritual cosmos. I use will almost exclusively in *acting*, in *doing* some deed in either the material or the spiritual world.

I use the effect of the will in the following way. When it has separated down into the lower part of the abdomen, then into the legs, into the feet and even into the earth, I lose much of the ability to act (as with both thinking and feeling). However, as soon as I let the will flow upwards again, this inability will change into its opposite. When the will, on its upward-flowing path, has reached the area of the abdomen, I meet it with a strong and intention-filled thought. In this mixed will-thought, the willpower then creates a force that flows out into the arms, the legs or into some other living entity in the outside world. This force can give strength to the arms, the legs or influence any outside living being. If I direct this force to an acupuncture point, this point will then be successfully treated. If I direct it to earth radiation, I can move this radiation or change it in some way.

With this force, we can influence many aspects of ourselves or others; we can perform physical tasks with great power, such as correcting a misaligned hip or neck, or we can hit a tennis ball at great speed or play a perfect tune on a flute.

*

According to Rudolf Steiner, humanity collectively passed 'the threshold' during the twentieth century. To my mind, this means that the separation of thinking, feeling and will is happening more or less to everybody. Also, as the three realms of the elemental world, with its more-or-less demonic inhabitants, also opened in 1879, 1949 and 2019 (as we will see later), the road through the adversarial domains is open, and *Ragnarok** is in full effect. This can lead to many strange experiences, even to frightening and inexplicable depressions or similar psychic conditions. Some spiritual scientists think that this will lead to more and more psychiatric epidemics. The only way out of this is to understand what is happening, but as materialistic medical science, especially psychiatry, today denies the existence of the spiritual world, this will be difficult.

---

* In Norse mythology, *Ragnarök*, described in the *Poetic Edda*, is a series of events, including a great battle foretold to lead to the death of a number of great figures (including the gods Odin, Thor, Týr, Freyr, Heimdallr and Loki), natural disasters and the submersion of the world in water. After these events, the world will resurface anew and fertile, the surviving and returning gods will meet and the world will be repopulated by human survivors.

Introduction

My intention with this book is to describe the crossing of the threshold according to the *Northern stream* of spirituality, and the *spiritual
realms* traversed through such a crossing, which are the three elemental realms, the 'inner' etheric world and the 'outer' etheric world. Further, I will describe my encounters with the guardian of the threshold
to the outer etheric world, who gave his names as Vidar and Balder.
I will also refer to the teachings of this guardian.

I will argue that the deeper realms of the elemental world have
opened gradually to the human race. People who are today search-
ing already live for much of the time in the three elemental realms,
and want to find this reality described and explained. Only by
traversing these three realms can we reach Christ, who is to be found
in the *'outer'* etheric world, a world that lies *'behind'* the three realms
of the elemental world. The etheric world can thus be found both
'outside' and 'inside' the elemental realms.

*

When we speak of a 'threshold', we should bear in mind that it is
not a definite line. It is more like a continuous change in your view
and understanding of a spiritual reality that is the foundation of the
totality of Creation – although there are certain 'areas' that feel more
like a distinct threshold.

On every step of this continuous threshold, we are presented with
a 'guardian' force or entity. The guardians of these thresholds are
more-or-less like a continuous meeting in all realms of physical, elemental and spiritual existence.

Here are some examples of guardians of the threshold:

1. The guardian of the spiritual world, also called the great guardian, often experienced as an Archangel or even Christ himself.
2. The guardian of the physical world, often the first that one
   meets for those following the Northern path.
3. The guardians of the elemental world – one's own creation,
   developed through the more-or-less correct understanding
   and observation of the higher spiritual world – even the
   elemental world.

4. The guardians of the demonic 'under-nature' or 'sub-natural' world. These are frightening and demonic entities, also often at least created partly by one's own deeds and thoughts, desires and wrong-doings.

5. The guardian of the outer etheric world, who presented himself to me as Vidar/Balder. This threshold was almost like a distinct line.

All of these thresholds are in turn threefold, and all of the guardians are in turn twofold.

*

When we die, we immediately pass such a distinct threshold, and we often enter into a part of the spiritual/etheric world, separated by or through a sort of dark tunnel-wall (as described by, among others, Dr Raymond Moody*), meeting the spiritual/etheric light and entities at the end of the tunnel – which can be described as our Angel, one or some of our deceased family-members, Christ or the greater guardian of the threshold.

This 'tunnel' has been of great importance and interest to me. In available literature, the focus and descriptions of this tunnel is only related to the 'inside', through which the newly-deceased person travels. Little is said about the wall of the tunnel itself, and even less about the outside of the tunnel.

I experience and view this wall as the elemental world, which is the creation of spiritual powers, consisting of the three elemental realms described later in this book. I see, define and experience both the inside and the outside of this tunnel-wall as the spiritual world 'within, beside or outside' material creation:

- I see the inside as the part of the spiritual world directly connected with material creation, as described in Greek or Nordic mythology. This part I see or experience as bright and flowing crystal water.
- My view of the outside of the tunnel is actually very different. I experience this as a part of the spiritual world that is more or less 'free' of material creation. I see or experience this aspect as

---

*Raymond A. Moody, Jr. (1944–) is a philosopher, psychologist, physician and author, most widely known for his books about life after death and near-death experiences (NDE), a term that he coined in 1975 in his bestselling book *Life After Life*.

woollen clouds, like a pastel-coloured cumulus creation. Personally, within these clouds I feel or see the possibility to meet Christ. The description in the Bible and the metaphor 'clouds' is, then, quite exact.*

'Beside' the tunnel is, in my experience, where the two etheric worlds meet – just where the tunnel ends. And two aspects strike me as being related to this division of the etheric world:

1. In the description of the ascension of Christ, it would seem that he left the 'inner' etheric world and took abode in the 'outer' etheric world.
2. In Genesis, it is described that God made two parts of the 'waters'. To me this resembles the 'inner' or 'under' parts of the etheric world, and the 'outer' or 'upper' part.†

Thus, the present book is about the three elemental kingdoms, which I find in the wall, the inner and outer etheric world and the different thresholds between the separate worlds or realms. The wall is a material creation, and to investigate this is our human obligation. The spiritual 'inside' the wall is a definite part of the spiritual world, relating to the creation of the wall itself. The spiritual 'outside' is our future spiritual existence, the Christ of the etheric world. This wall is experienced, as most 'things' in the material, elemental and spiritual world, as threefold.

*

There are three realms constituting the elemental world, the wall of the tunnel.

- The third elemental realm.
- The second elemental realm.
- The first elemental realm.

If the dead person travelling through the tunnel has been initiated (or partly initiated) whilst on earth, he/she may also (have to) work

---

*John describes this scene as Jesus returns: 'Behold, he is coming with the clouds, and every eye will see him, even those who pierced him, and all tribes of the earth will wail on account of him. Even so. Amen.' (Revelation 1:7.)

†See the description from the elves in this book (p. 72), and also the quotes from the Bible on p. 72.

through (at least parts of) this wall – those parts that he/she has been conscious about, has 'understood' – and thus traverses several of the thresholds and meets several of the guardians.

When as living beings we cross the first threshold, we usually do not go through the tunnel as we do when we die, but we make our way through *the wall* of the tunnel, this dark wall which I will call the *elemental* world. The un-initiated human being will at first experience this world or realm as total darkness.

I will describe or define this elemental world as the sum total of the forces and beings that are the living foundation of the material world.* Every little drop, atom, flower or cloud that we think is the material world is just an illusion, an image of the real living powers that are behind the material world. Without the elemental world, there would be no material world. The elemental world thus contains the spiritual helpers that enable us to experience material existence. They are our friends. (Some elemental forces and entities that have abandoned earth development may be found in the interior of the earth, where also some of the dead were found when Christ liberated them during his descent into the depths of the earth, between his death and resurrection.)

*

The first entity that I meet in the 'outside' etheric world is a joyful entity, high up at my right side. At my question of who 'he' is, he presents himself as 'Vidar'. This is very interesting, as Vidar is known to be the 'presenter' of Christ in the etheric world. He is described traditionally (in Nordic mythology) as the one god to survive the great battle of *Ragnarök*, and is the outer and shining aura of Christ himself. He also continues the work of Michael as an Archangel, since Michael became elevated to the rank of an Archai. (This meeting with Vidar will be discussed in Chapter 1.)

*

Rudolf Steiner recounts the beginning of our evolution by reminding us that our human soul contained, from the start, a powerful primeval

---

* The material cosmos has as such three realms or levels of creation, which I can view or experience as 'three mothers'. This resembles the philosophy of Pherecydes of Cyros, who was not only the first Greek philosopher but also the last cosmological poet, and he differentiates between three original principles, three archetypical mothers from whom creation has been formed.

wisdom. But in the beginning the seed of this wisdom had to be nurtured to achieve the spiritual heights we needed to attain in order to become developed beings in a material existence. We needed a spiritual guide from the higher hierarchies to assist us in the growth of our 'I'-consciousness. This teacher was the fallen archangel called Lucifer.

Lucifer incarnated in the flesh in China around 3,000 years before Christ, a short time after the onset of the Dark Age, Kali Yuga, and laid the foundations of an intellectual age.[*] According to Steiner, Ahriman will incarnate in the West, 2-3,000 years after the incarnation of Christ, in the 'first part' of the third millennium. To 'incarnate' does not necessarily mean to be 'born' in the usual way, however. Paul Emberson believed that Ahriman could incarnate through the world wide web and, through these means, work through individuals (for example in role-playing online games such as the fantasy 'World of Warcraft').

The Azuras work in the consciousness soul and the 'I'. To understand the forces and work of the Azuras, we have to look to the beginning of the twenty-first century. Rudolf Steiner generally avoided this subject in his lectures, and I believe the reason for this was that the realm of Azuras, which is the first elemental realm, was not fully 'opened' until around 2019. Of course, this doesn't mean that an initiate like Steiner did not have access to this realm, but that ordinary individuals who are able to travel the expanses of the spiritual world could not. If we enter areas that are not yet truly 'open' to our consciousness (as with the use of drugs), we may end up insane. That is why, in my view, Steiner advised the painter Hilma af Klint[†] to restrict her spiritual voyages somewhat, as it seems that her pictures were taken from the second realm of the elemental world, which was not truly 'open' until around 1949.

---

[*]This is described in my book *The Lucifer Deception*, Clairview Books 2020.

[†]Hilma af Klint (1862–1944) was a Swedish artist and mystic whose paintings were the first Western abstract works known to the current art community. A considerable body of her work predates the first purely abstract compositions by Kandinsky. Her paintings, which sometimes resemble diagrams, were a visual representation of complex spiritual ideas.

I have often observed luciferic entities, as well as ahrimanic entities, as I do this regularly when working with sick animals and humans. The luciferic entities and forces are always situated at the upper or cranial part of the patient. They are bright, attractive, loquacious and witty. They are related to intelligence, talking, the nervous system and light. They are aligned to the 'up-down' axis and are related to diseases of the nervous system.

The ahrimanic entities and forces are always situated at the lower, distal or caudal part of the patient. They are silent, somewhat dark, strong and piercing. They are related to the flesh and the bones of the body. They are aligned to the 'right-left' axis, and are related to diseases of the dense tissues.

In the middle, between the luciferic and the ahrimanic forces, I see the Christ force, or maybe even the Christ himself, situated somewhat towards the luciferic entity, that is, a little proximal or cranial to the Middle point. The Christ force is not aligned with any axis as such.

The azuric entities or forces, which I never saw before 2019, are situated in the middle of the body, somewhat to the right and below the Christ force. The arithmetical middle is thus between the Azuras and the Christ. They are related to the blood, and I see them as coagulated blood, pouring forth. They become stronger and visible when the person carrying them engages in lies that encompass the whole of humanity (not personal lies).

Oil painting by Are Thoresen

*

The Representative of Man, Rudolf Steiner's wooden sculpture

Regarding Steiner's wooden sculpture 'The Representative of Man', this monumental work of art elegantly sums up the plight and redemption of mankind. Studying it gives me many insights regarding treatment with 'the Christ point'. The exact Middle point, where Lucifer and Ahriman join their hands, lies just below the level of the heart of Christ. However, in this sculpture, there are several more secrets to be found. These are secrets that may reveal, strengthen and make clear the therapeutic possibilities that we can utilize to combat and transform these demons. These are some of my insights obtained from studying this statue:

1. Beginning with the obvious, Christ is the dividing force between Lucifer and Ahriman.
2. The cooperation or combination of these two forces poses a serious threat to humankind.
3. The luciferic and the ahrimanic forces join below the heart of Christ (and for that matter, man).
4. There are two Ahrimans and two Lucifers, so that the meeting points between them in the body are in two places, one under the heart and one at the level of the throat.
5. The 'Cosmic Humour' (in the top corner) appears where a group is gathered, in celebration of the healing force of Christ.

This structure should, in my view, be incorporated in our thinking, feeling and will. Only then will we be able to gain or access any dominion over the three occultisms.*

- Through the feeling/imagination over 'hygienic occultism', related to the third realm of the elemental world.
- Through the thinking/inspiration over 'mechanical occultism', related to the second realm of the elemental world.
- Through the will/intuition over 'eugenic occultism', related to the first realm of the elemental world.

*

Returning to the threshold, it should be said that the expression 'other side' is somewhat wrong, for in the spiritual world there

---

* See Appendix 2 for an extended description from Rudolf Steiner on these three 'occultisms'.

is no distance and no time, at least as we know it in the material world. That said, there are several layers, areas or levels of consciousness on the other side of the threshold. After crossing, one may, by divine grace, be transported to higher realms of the spiritual world, to higher angelic worlds, but it seems to me – also by reading what others have described – that the most common or usual outcome is that we first meet the elemental world, specifically the third realm of the elemental world, and often especially the more demonic part of this world or realm. This is also what I have met, with few exceptions.

As described, the threshold itself is multifaceted, and may be likened to walking through a large forest. The path followed is full of smaller and larger stones and holes, bends and hills. In my experience, the biggest 'hole' is between the material world and the third realm of the elemental world. Between the third realm and the second realm, the hole is smaller, and between the second and the first it is somewhat in between. The threshold between the elemental world and the pure outer etheric world is very different and much 'softer'.

This is probably why there are so many diverse opinions, observations and concepts about the elemental world:

- Some call it the spiritual world (which is true to some extent, as it is not strictly material, but is only the foundation of the material deception or illusion).
- Some call it the etheric world (which is true to some extent, as the beings and entities living there, as well as those living in the material world, use etheric 'energy' to be alive).
- Some call it the demonic world (which is true to some extent, as this demonic part is often the first area of the elemental world that we enter).
- Some call it the world of elves (which is true to some extent, as the third realm of the elemental world is home to all kinds of nature beings).
- And (as I do), some call it the elemental world...

When we pass the first threshold into the elemental world, it is important that we understand a little about what this elemental world really is. The elemental world is the sum of those spiritual forces that have made it possible for the illusion of material substances to appear to the human mind. To make this possible, the three angelic realms needed the cooperation of the three realms of what we now call adversarial forces or entities. These entities are labelled 'adversarial' because they are the foundation of the material illusion, and thus may lead us into error. These three forces are the luciferic, the ahrimanic and the azuric forces or entities.

The elemental world has been created successively during the whole material experience of the earthly realm, starting with Old Saturn, Old Sun, Old Moon and today's Earth.* There are thus, as with most celestial phenomena, three levels of the elemental world:

- The third realm, containing the spiritual blueprint of myriad nature forms as well as the invisible elemental beings of nature.
- The second realm, containing the structure or blueprint of atoms.
- The first realm, containing the structure of cosmic vacuum.

In mastering the forces of these three realms, we can develop a certain power over these entities, thus, as we have seen, creating three forms of occult powers, 'hygienic occultism', 'mechanical occultism' and 'eugenic occultism'.

In the development of the human mind, this mind will penetrate the great illusion of materiality and understand the forces

---

*In anthroposophy, the concept of astronomy reaches far beyond the material concept of the universe we have been taught by science. The planets to which Steiner refers represent much more than the material rock and gaseous formations we observe in our telescopes – they represent real spiritual beings. What we are also unable to directly observe is that these planets also represent different phases of the evolution of the entire universe, including ourselves. Therefore, according to anthroposophy, at the beginning of time the solar system was in a planetary phase called Old Saturn. So far there have been four incarnations of our system: Old Saturn, Old Sun, Old Moon and the present Earth that we currently inhabit. Our current planet is a culmination of the previous stages of cosmic evolution as part of the continued evolution of the entire solar system. Between each phase of evolution, there is a death or a pause, followed by a 'reincarnation' into a new form. After the present Earth stage of evolution, the cosmos will dissolve then rest, after which everything in the solar system will reincarnate in a new condition called 'Future Jupiter'. This process of creation, dissolution and rest will be repeated in two more phases: 'Future Venus' and 'Future Vulcan'.

behind, thus liberating the entities of the three realms of the elemental world:

- The third realm is liberated by developing feeling, the astral body and thus becoming Manas* (spirit self).
- The second realm is liberated by developing and controlling thinking, the etheric body and thus becoming Buddhi (spirit self).
- The first realm is liberated by developing and controlling will, the physical body and thus becoming Atma (spirit man).

*

After crossing the threshold into the elemental world, I experience three paths:

- The path into the *third realm*, as well as the third angelic realm. This is the way that Rudolf Steiner describes in his Helsinki lectures of 3 & 4 April 1912.[†] (I also believe that this is the path of the First Class of the School of Spiritual Science.)
- The path into the *second realm*, as well as the second angelic realm, the archangelic realm. Rudolf Steiner described this path in the lecture he gave in Torquay, England, on 15 August 1924.[‡] (Could this also be the way that was later to be described in the Second Class of the School of Spiritual Science – not given due to Rudolf Steiner's death in 1925?)
- The path into the *first realm*, as well as the first angelic realm, the archaic realm. Rudolf Steiner described this way in his

---

*In Steiner's description of human beings, he categorizes our make-up using several methods. First, he divides us into four layers, consisting of our physical, etheric, astral and 'I' sheaths. However, this concept of a fourfold being can be further described as having both seven and even nine levels, if one also considers our spiritual future as including the higher levels named Manas, Buddhi and Atma. Ultimately, our higher selves, as well as all of creation, are governed by a primary trinity of the powerful soul faculties of thinking, feeling and will. They represent the fundamental processes in which our cosmos is organized and developed, and weave themselves into all aspects of creation.

[†]*Spiritual Beings in the Heavenly Bodies and in the Kingdoms of Nature*, op. cit.

[‡]*True and False Paths in Spiritual Research*, Rudolf Steiner Press 2020.

lectures held in Dornach, Switzerland on 5 & 12 July 1924.* (And, could it be that this was a first hint of the content to be given in the future Third Class of the School of Spiritual Science?)

*

One important question that the honoured reader may ask is why the elemental realms, as well as the different etheric worlds, have not been described in greater detail before now? It is of the utmost importance to understand that our access to both the elemental realms and the etheric worlds is constantly changing.

All things are in a certain development – development of the spiritual or elemental reality. Even material reality is in development, as well as the political, economic, psychological or geographical reality of the world or cosmos. Everything is always in a process of development and change. What existed yesterday, in relation to all those parameters, is different today. All things must change, and nothing ever repeats itself.

One important thing that changes, too, is human consciousness, as well as occult abilities, degrees of clairvoyance and the successive opening of the spiritual world. In 1879, the spirits of darkness entered our material/elemental realm; in 1899 the Dark Age (Kali Yuga) ended, and between 1918 and 1933 it became possible to see Christ in the etheric world. The time of the consciousness soul is dawning, and the accessibility of the elemental realms is progressing.

According to my research, the threefold fundamentals of material creation are now slowly opening to human experience:

1. The third realm of the elemental world has been completely open to humans since around 1879.
2. The second realm of the elemental world has been completely open to humans since around 1949, 70 years after the first opening.
3. The first realm of the elemental world has been completely open to humans since around 2019, again 70 years after the second opening.

These dates are of course only approximate.

*

* See Rudolf Steiner, *Esoteric Lessons for the First Class of the School of Spiritual Science at the Goetheanum, Volumes One to Four*, Rudolf Steiner Press 2020.

- The 'inner' etheric world is a creation by the Gods to nourish their creation, which is the wall of the 'tunnel'.
- The 'outer' etheric world is the home of the Gods.
- The 'elemental' world, with its three realms, is created by the angelic hierarchies in cooperation with the so-called adversarial forces.

1. The third realm is associated mainly with the luciferic forces and entities in cooperation with the Angels.
2. The second realm is associated mainly with the ahrimanic forces and entities in cooperation with the Archangels.
3. The first realm is associated mainly with the azuric forces and entities in cooperation with the Archai.

The opening of the third realm of the elemental world was closely connected to the ending of the Dark Age, so-called Kali Yuga. The opening of the second realm of the elemental world was closely connected to the start of the 'atomic' age. The opening of the first realm is closely connected to the Covid-19 pandemic.* These openings change the world to a certain degree and also partly ourselves – at least for those who can observe these changes.

- As the third realm has to do with the elemental beings of nature, I would presume that there would have been less 'growth-power' and regeneration in trees and plants (although I cannot prove this).
- As the second realm has much to do with molecules and atoms, especially in transelementation,† several biodynamic farmers observed a change in the effect of biodynamic preparations at

---

* Since ancient times, initiation or travelling into the spiritual worlds was linked to some kind of unconsciousness, to weakening of the body or disease. The teacher of Dante, Brunetto Latini, based much of his insights and teachings on what he experienced during heat stroke, when he met the Goddess Natura (Demeter). Personally, I have always enjoyed having the flu, as this brought me into the spiritual world. To go through infection from Covid-19 was essential to all my writings on the elemental and etheric realms and worlds. A vaccination against these diseases (coronaviruses and flu) would then (in my view) also be a vaccination against spiritual thinking and experiences. It would be considered a small victory for Ahriman.

† Or transubstantiation.

this time. Several even thought the preparations had lost all their power during this period.

- As the first realm has to do with the vacuum of both matter and space, including the interior of the sun, the change here will concern the 'I'-forces of the human being. This is a spiritual portal, and this change is connected to Covid-19, and reveals its azuric dragon-forces.

During the years 2020-21, I was engaged in working through these three realms, between which there are lesser thresholds. Between the first realm of the elemental world and the outer etheric world, we meet the next major threshold, where today we may find the Christ.

*

During Rudolf Steiner's life, especially during the time of his delivery of the nineteen lessons of the First Class of the School of Spiritual Science,* only the third elemental realm was 'open' to the ordinary human being. This realm is described in Steiner's sixth lecture of the above, but he indicates the other two in the seventh. Those that were able to penetrate into the second or first realm, were advised by Steiner to refrain from doing so (as I mentioned with the Swedish artist, Hilma af Klint).

Today, in my opinion, it is of the utmost importance to understand the three elemental realms, because we have to traverse these realms in order to reach the outer etheric world where Christ may be found, and also to be able to master the spiritual dominance of the physical world, or else we will leave this mastery to the adversarial forces and entities.

The opening of the first elemental realm, and the subsequent access to the outer etheric world, is in my opinion one of the most important incidents of the twenty-first century. If we are unable to introduce our good will and Christian heart into this first elemental realm, it will be lost to the 'I'-devastating work of the azuric forces.

After exploration of the third, second and first elemental realms, the outside of the tunnel may also be explored. Here we can find a spiritual reality quite different to the etheric reality inside the tunnel. I have had some time to explore this outer realm of the etheric world

---

* See Rudolf Steiner, *Esoteric Lessons for the First Class of the School of Spiritual Science at the Goetheanum*, op. cit.

lately, so I can offer some personal descriptions. I have met and conversed with the guardian of the threshold of this outer etheric world, and I have likewise caught some insights in – and glimpses of – the etheric land of this region, as will be described later.

As I have said, it is only when we have worked our way through the three elemental realms that we can reach the etheric world outside the tunnel, and it is only here that the Christ can be found. Thus, the 'time is at hand'!

*

The three adversarial groups, together with the angelic realms of the third hierarchy, have actually given us the possibility to exist in the material world, this mirror or illusion of the elemental world.

It is also important to remember that the whole of the elemental world is 'fuelled' by etheric forces, originating in the etheric world, which may be characterized as being 'beyond' the elemental worlds (both inside and outside, but mainly inside).

In the third and partly the second realm of the elemental world, we can find the 'commonly described' demonic worlds, especially the adversarial forces and entities of the etheric realm related to health and disease.* We also find all the nature beings, such as the tree-fairies and the flower-fairies. If we can master these entities or powers, we can practice 'hygienic occultism'. That is, to influence or heal the spiritual causes of disease in a spiritual, magical or occult way. These powers or abilities will be important when both ordinary medicine and plant medicine start to lose their power, which to a large degree they already have. We can also master or influence the processes of nature, as well as weather and other natural phenomena. In this realm one breathes darkness, not air, and all is dominated by 'forms'.

In the second and partly the third and the first realm, in this 'deeper' realm of the elemental world, we find or meet the elemental beings related to material substances, molecules and atoms. If we can master these entities or powers, we can practice 'mechanical occultism'. That is, to influence the spiritual causes of material objects or machines in a magical or occult way. This will be very important when, in the future, machines will carry the evil principle of the adversarial forces,

---

* In all three elemental realms there are also deeper and darker aspects of the demonic, lingering in the deep layers of the earth. These are pure evil and will not be dealt with or described here.

or may even threaten to overtake the world. The Philosopher's Stone, which can master the transubstantiation of elements, must take its powers from this realm. This realm is dominated by colours and light, although a much sharper light than we find in the etheric world. In this second realm, one breathes colours and light.

In the first realm, in this even deeper realm of the elemental world, we encounter even more powerful elemental beings, the bringers of death and birth, related to the 'empty' space between the so-called atomic or elementary particles. If we can master these powers we can practice 'eugenic occultism'. This will be of the utmost importance around the year 6,000, when Rudolf Steiner prophesized that women will lose their natural ability for conception and pregnancy. We need to learn to influence the spiritual causes of birth and death in a magical way, as well as the enormous powers found in the vacuum. In this realm, one breathes energy or force, and all is dominated by strength and force.

The three realms here described are to a certain extent interconnected. The adversarial beings appear in all the three realms, as well as the physical/material bodies of all entities created, but they appear to be totally different in the three realms.

In the different types of occultism mentioned, there are two ways of dealing with them:

- Left-hand occultism, or expressed differently, *black magic*. Black magic violates the sovereignty and untouchability of the free 'I' of the human being.
- Right-hand occultism, or expressed differently, *white magic*. White magic does not violate the sovereignty and untouchability of the free 'I' of the human being.

Of course, we want to avoid black magic and choose white magic, by bringing morality and the power of Christ into our choices and work.

According to Rudolf Steiner, our physical world is in its death process, and before too long (6,000 years) we will not be able to survive without mastering the elemental realms, that is, without mastering the three different occultisms. This is a must!

*

The elemental beings in all three realms of the elemental world are the 'true' foundation of the material universe (although this 'true' foundation is also an illusion, the greater *maya*). Without them, the material world would not exist.

We should thus understand that the 'materiality' of the cosmos represents the adversarial forces: Ahriman, Lucifer and the Azuras, as well as the angelic hierarchies. Material creation is thus the outer face or expression of the elemental beings of all the three realms of the elemental world, which are to be categorized as (partly) adversarial, but necessary to our human development towards freedom.

I must also add that the elemental beings are of two kinds, two main groups. There are the ones that do their rightful work in creating the material world, and those that are backwards or retarded and act as 'rebels' – that work and create in 'wrong' places and processes, seducing the minds of genuinely seeking individuals and spiritual beings and helping other and greater demons.

*

All elemental beings of all three realms of the elemental world are of partly adversarial origin by definition, and may be categorized as 'evil',* although Rudolf Steiner calls only those of birth and death (belonging to the first elemental realm) genuinely evil, as they derive from the azuric forces, to which also Sorat, the Sun Demon, belongs.

In my view, to be able to develop and influence all of the above categories of elemental being, it is essential for us to be able to see them, to observe them and also gain power by breathing the elements of that particular elemental realm, which must be done with a deep and heartfelt Christ-consciousness. We can also try to 'insert' Christ by 'opening' the Middle point. To me, this is necessary in developing mechanical, hygienic and eugenic occultism.

In summary, it is necessary to:

- observe the elemental beings by some kind of supersensible method;
- breathe the element in which these elemental beings live:
  - third realm, 'structured-coloured-light';
  - second realm, 'vibrational-coloured-light';
  - first realm, 'radiant-coloured-light';
- open the realm, or especially the material creations of this particular realm, to the Christ force by opening the Middle point between Lucifer and Ahriman/Azuras.

---

* The elemental beings can be transformed by the power of Christ, and are then no longer 'evil'.

We must learn to know and observe the elemental beings or forces of:

- The third elemental realm, so that we can help to heal diseases of the world, as described for *hygienic occultism*.
- The second elemental realm, so that we can help to heal the mechanical system of the world, as described for *mechanical occultism*.
- The first elemental realm, so that we can help to heal the system of death and birth, as described for *eugenic occultism*.

*

The adversarial or elemental forces exist in everybody and everything, and when they get too strong, too unbalanced, or appear in the wrong place or at the wrong time, they will create:

- disease (relating to the third elemental realm);
- adversarial technology (relating to the second elemental realm);
- and manipulated birth and death (relating to the first elemental realm).

As a doctor, I usually observe, through my clairvoyant abilities, the disease forces or demons of the third realm of the elemental world, and sometimes also the third realm of the third angelic hierarchy. I watch how the luciferic, ahrimanic and also the azuric spirits appear and behave, and also react to what the patient says or tells me. I also observe the distance between the different demonic powers, as this is where the healing can be activated, in the form of the Christ force.

How these spirits look and behave can give several clues for therapy, for example:

- In a patient with longstanding bronchitis, I was able to see how the luciferic adversarial spirit reacted differently with different kinds of external heat:
  - when heat from burning firewood was applied (sitting in front of the fireplace), the adversarial spirit was weakened greatly;
  - with heated water, heated by electricity, the adversarial spirit was weakened less;
  - with sunlight directly from the sun, the adversarial spirit was considerably weakened.

- In a patient with a chronic digestive problems, I put different healing plants over the stomach and watched how the ahrimanic adversarial spirit became weakened.
- In a patient with psychiatric problems, I watched how the Christ force of the Middle grew or strengthened itself differently, according to my own mentality, my own humility, and of how much 'etheric life' I was able to project through this humility.
- In a patient with different medical problems, and who was also a strong follower and believer in so-called 'conspiracy theories', I observed how the azuric forces or entities moved or gained strength as the patient started to tell me about his theories.

*

The three realms of the elemental world are divided in different sub-layers:

- the third realm is mainly related to the elementals of earth, water, air, fire (the classical elements are four categories);
- the second realm is mainly related to the different layers (there are ten groups of material elements, thus ten categories);
- the first realm to the vacuum of reality, the birth place of the elemental particles (there are presently seventeen elemental particles, thus seventeen categories).

*

The release or liberation of the imprisoned elemental beings of the three realms and the use of their etheric forces in the construction of our own spiritual forces, is another aspect of the development of our earthly existence.

- The liberation of the beings of the third realm seem to be connected to the dying or destruction of the *forms* of all the nature beings, especially by death (Rudolf Steiner described this in the gradual dying-off of butterfly and bird species).
- The liberation of the beings of the second realm seem to be connected to the changing of the molecules, as when compounds are split in digestion (which releases disease-creating ahrimanic elementals), or as when C and O combines to CO_2 in the metabolism and blood-lung-system of man,

creating health-giving elementals (Steiner describes this in several places in relation to our digestion or the production of food in agriculture).

- The liberation of the beings of the first realm seem to be connected to the coming and going of the elementary particles, born out of the cosmic vacuum.

Through the ability to step over the threshold of all three realms using the techniques described in this book (the Northern path), and realizing that all creation is threefold, with Lucifer on the one side, Ahriman and/or the Azuras on the other side (the adversarial forces at the extremes) and the Christ-force in the Middle, I have come to develop techniques (finding 'the Middle') that can diminish or totally remove the strength of the adversarial beings in pathology, as well as pathological influences we might be influenced by, for example electro-magnetic radiation.

It is my firm belief that this way should also be the method if we are to be able to control the powers of the material world, and thus develop the moral path to atmospheric or meteorological, as well as to hygienic, mechanical and eugenic occultism.

To deal with and diminish the actions and powers of the adversarial forces today is of the utmost importance for the survival of the human race. In all these forces, in all man-made devices and even in all human abilities, there can be found a Middle point, the Christ force. By finding this, we can redeem the luciferic, ahrimanic and (hopefully) the azuric elements of all the described forces, devices, processes, and consequently material reality itself.

The Christ force or Christ consciousness can be found:

- In the electro-magnetic forces, in the middle of feeling, between sympathy and antipathy.
- In the nuclear forces, in the middle of thinking, between dead thinking and living thinking, between matter and anti-matter.
- In the gravitational forces, in the middle of will, between gravity and anti-gravity (anti-gravity has not yet been discovered, but science believes it exists).
- In the vacuum-force, related to the Azuras; also in the middle, in the middle of 'nothing-ness'.

In influencing matter, whether it be in the realms of birth, death, machines, electro-magnetic radiation, weather or health—as all of these have their invisible foundations in the existence of elemental beings—we have to be able to manipulate, concentrate and use our own forces of thinking, feeling and will, and insert them into the Middle region of all these processes – Christ in me – Christ in them – Christ in all.

To be able to work into and with the elemental world in all its three realms, to introduce morality and the Christ-force in the material/elemental world, we have to be able to *observe* the elemental world. That is why it is so important today to be able to cross the threshold (to the spiritual world), and also to be able to activate one or more of our spiritual sense organs.

On all levels, the adversarial forces can mislead you, fool you, cheat you and corrupt you. They can corrupt your senses and your morals, they can send a parasitic host into your body to make you think, falsely, that you are clairvoyant (see later), and they can conceal the Christ-force in your heart. All this must be avoided and, calmly, rejected.

*

As we have seen, in relation to the passing of the threshold, we will always meet, in some form, the phenomenon or entity called 'the guardian of the threshold'.

This meeting, and the abyss between the material world and that world which this entity guards, might be somewhat different according to which path we follow over the threshold, whether it be the Northern, Southern or Middle path, as well as the thinking path, the feeling path or the will path. Also, it seems to me that this experience changes definitely during the progression of time and humanity's situation in general. The guardian is also different on the different thresholds.

The guardian of the threshold stands before the abyss in order to remind us of the dangers, and to instruct us what to do and what not to do when passing it. Sometimes, if we are not mature enough, we simply cannot pass, and must wait until a later time. However, if we are mature and ripe enough to cross the threshold, we may not meet the guardian at all.

At a certain level, time and maturity, we meet three 'animals', as a reminder of what we need to change within ourselves in order to make a safe crossing. Rudolf Steiner described our three 'soul forces', and the parts of them that have not been mastered, as three animals:

- one crooked, bluish and skeletonized, that represents the mistakes and faults in our will;
- one ugly and lying, yellowish creature that represents the mistakes and faults in our feeling; and
- one sneering, reddish creature with bared teeth, that represents the faults and errors in our thinking.

Steiner says that these animals can also be perceived as:*

- A dragon (the Door of the Sun) in the will.
- A huge lion (the Door of the Elements) in the feeling.
- A flying head with wings (the Door of Death) in the thinking.

The Vikings knew about the existence of these three animals, or soul forces, that had to be acknowledged and transformed before one could reach the spiritual world in safety. They described the way over to the spiritual world as a bridge – *Hjallarbrui* – and the three animals that hindered you in passing as:

- A bull that tried to head-butt you (this happened when you had not mastered your will).
- A snake that tried to bite you (this happened when you had not mastered your feeling).
- A dog that tried to bite you (this happened when you had not mastered your thinking).

If we don't prepare ourselves by training our feeling, thinking and will, we will not be able to experience the good spiritual forces, but instead will be led down pathways of illusion by the adversaries.

A peculiarity of the Northern way is that it leads us to confront the three animals in the *external, material world*. If we look through the illusion of materiality, we will meet them in the three realms of the elemental world, mirroring into the material world in form, structure and force.

---

* See lecture held on 2 March 1915 (*Menschenschicksale und Völkerschicksale*, GA 157).

Chapter 1

Meeting Vidar and Balder
Beyond the Elemental Realms

In my post-Covid-19 exhaustion, I was sitting on the sofa in front of my fireplace, feeling half dead. I attempted to travel to the first realm of the elemental world, in order to carry out investigations. In my weakness, however, I did not have the power to stop at the first realm, and found myself at its farthest border. This border made a very strange impression, as if it was moving and changing in a manner that I had never seen before.

I crossed the border and entered a whole new world – a world that at first glance appeared like a mirror reflection of the totality of both the material, the inner etheric and also the three realms of the elemental world. However, the colours and movements in this new world were not like the colours in either the material world or the elemental realms. They were like a pastel-coloured water or jelly.

I recalled from my studies on the life after death that, on many levels, one gets the choice between two options, two different roads:

- One is characterized by strong light and strong colours.
- The other is characterized by soft light and pastel-soft colours.

The road with the strong light, colours and sounds leads to the adversarial forces of the elemental realm, especially to Lucifer.

The road with the soft light, colours and sounds leads to the Christ-forces of the etheric realm, to Christ.[*]

I became convinced that this was the 'real' etheric world. I will try to explain further, in my own words, how to differentiate between the etheric world and the three elemental worlds, and also the further astral and devachanic worlds that lie 'behind' or 'above' the etheric world.

---

[*] It is interesting to note that the Tibetan *Book of the Dead* instructs you to choose the strong light at every 'road-crossing' on the way to heaven after death. That is why the Buddhists are often called 'the Children of Lucifer'.

The etheric forces are almost everywhere, penetrating and filling both the material world, the three realms of the elemental world, and of course the etheric world itself.

This etheric force or power gives life to all creation, material and non-material.

In the material world, as also in the elemental world, this 'etheric energy' is used by all living beings. This means that even trolls* use etheric energy in order to act.

Many who cross the threshold and enter the world behind it, mistake the elemental world for the etheric world. To make the distinction between the pure – which I will call the 'outer' – etheric world and the elemental world, is thus of crucial importance.

In the elemental world WE have to bring in the Christ.

In the etheric world we are able to MEET the Christ.

The outer etheric world is both threefold, fourfold, sevenfold and twelvefold. The different streams or compartments of this world are differentiated by colours. All the colours are pastel, not shining or radiating as in the material world, partly in the inner etheric world and of course in the elemental world.

Unfortunately, I find numerous references by spiritual writers (even anthroposophists) that mix together these different worlds or realms. Often, the third elemental realm is described as the whole elemental world, the second realm as the etheric world and the first realm as the spiritual world or lower Devachan.† Then, the astral world may be mistaken for the higher devachanic world.

Already, I can sense that there are further worlds, which I presume are the astral world and then the spiritual and devachanic worlds.

*

---

*In Old Norse sources, beings described as trolls dwell in isolated rocks, mountains, or caves, live together in small family units, and are rarely helpful to human beings. (Hence the notion of an 'internet troll'!)

†Devachan has several divisions: the continents; the rivers and oceans; the airy region; etheric space; and the region of spiritual archetypes. In the first division everything is seen as though in a photographic negative. Everything physical that has ever existed on this Earth, whether as mineral, plant or animal, and everything physical that still exists, appears as a negative. And if you see yourself in this negative form, as one among all the others, you will be in Devachan.

When I cross the threshold, into the third elemental realm, then further to the second and the first realm, I have the definite impression that in addition to going 'deeper' into the spiritual, I also go 'higher' into the spiritual world, and also backwards as well as forwards in time.

Many have written about how to experience the etheric world, for example through sacred geometry. In my opinion, this is the elemental world, not the etheric. Thus, many descriptions of the etheric world will need to be reconsidered and re-evaluated.

*

Let us return to my living room and the soapstone fireplace, as the scene of travels into the three elemental realms and also the etheric worlds behind them – both the 'inner' and the 'outer' parts or realms of those worlds. Sitting there, I was contemplating my journeys when, for the first time, I was confronted with the guardian entity of the outer etheric realm. This was a huge, kind, childlike and smiling being, lingering high up at my right side. At my question of who 'he' was, he presented himself as 'Vidar', and in the same moment indicated that he also was very close to 'Balder'.

As already mentioned, as Vidar is known to be the 'presenter' of Christ in the etheric world. He is described traditionally as the one god to survive *Ragnarok*, the silent Ase (Åsagud), and according to some interpretations, the former protecting Angel of Buddha, the present Angel related to Buddha's Nirmanakaya (the astral-etheric soul of Buddha) – the keeper of the Nathan soul (the soul of the Nathan Jesus child, as described in the Luke gospel) and the outer and shining aura of Christ himself. He also continues the work of Michael as an Archangel, after Michael became elevated to the rank of Archai.

As a strictly personal comment, I must add that his appearance looked very much like the 'Cosmic Humour' presented in the wooden sculpture made by Rudolf Steiner and Edith Maryon (the 'Representative of Man' or 'the Group', see photo on p. 16). Another interesting aspect of this encounter is that it is apparent that the entities of Vidar and Balder are closely related, almost like twin spirits.

*

So, who is Balder? In Scandinavian mythology he is a god associated with light, beauty, love, poetry and happiness. According to the

Gylfaginning (the first part of the *Prose Edda*), Balder is the son of Odin and Frigg and married to Nanna with whom he has a son, Forsete. Balder lives in Breidablik (Norway), 'the place with a wide view'.

Balder had the most beautiful ship of all, the Ringhorne, on which he was cremated. The historian and poet Snorri Sturluson (1179–1241) wrote of Balder in his book on gods and quatrains, *The Younger Edda*, as follows:

> Balder is Odin's son, and there is much good to be said about him; he is the best and he praises everyone. He is so beautiful in appearance and so bright that he shines; yes, one special flower is so white that it is compared to the eyelashes of Balder [Balder-brå, Norse name, Mayweed or Tripleurospermum inodorum]. It is the whitest of all herbs, and from this you can understand how beautiful he is in both hair and body.

Sturluson portrays Balder as a gentle and good god, almost too good for this world, and the only negativity related to him is his murder by the blind god, Höd. Mediated by the ambiguous god Loki, it is the foremost sign or warning of the end times, *Ragnarok*.

Balder is a passive god, with no visible sign of a cult, and apparently leaving no imprint in terms of place names. Some say that Balder is the Nordic name for Christ. Vidar, then, is the outer layer or 'sheet' – the presenter and protector of Balder. Thus, they presented themselves to me almost as a singular being.

During the first weeks, the same 'progression' occurred, as always happens when I meet spiritual entities.* At first, I only see them – they don't observe me. Then, they slowly start to observe me, and in a way they mirror myself. This process usually takes a few weeks. Then, slowly, I can observe a sort of recognition in their eyes – they become friendlier, more filled with life. Then, after still more time has passed – it could be weeks or even months – they start to show me things or even start to communicate, like a living entity, like a friend.

---

* This development is to me quite similar to the whole creational development, from Old Saturn through Old Sun, Old Moon and then Earth. First, there is a pure presence, then this becomes penetrated with etheric life, then creation starts mirroring the cosmos and then it becomes full of conscious life.

Soon, I had reached the point where 'the' spiritual entity started to contact me with his 'eyes', and also showed me details of his surroundings. What Vidar showed me was quite unexpected... He revealed that behind him, and at his side, there were many other spiritual beings, looking somewhat similar, but smaller, actually in varying sizes. Again, I was left only to watch, to observe.

At this point, something interesting happened. I sent the unedited manuscript of this book, as it stood at that point, to two friends. Immediately, the Vidar entity became much more serious, almost as if he was reprimanding me. (Maybe spiritual encounters should be kept secret, at least for a while...?)

After that moment, the face of this spiritual entity became more structured and, in a way, older. It lost its babylike face, its childlike face, and took on the face of an older man. This development continued over the following days, and the face of this spiritual entity became older until its skin began to crack!

One morning, the face of this entity that called himself Vidar began to 'break'. It fell apart, in many pieces. The shock of this stayed with me, but then a new reality dawned, and a very deep mystery revealed itself before my eyes – a mystery I still can't unravel or understand properly.

Behind his face, or rather inside his 'body', another spiritual being appeared. Before I will describe this other being, I will try to say some words about the mystery of how the death of one entity, or insight or consciousness, is a necessity for the appearance or development of another, often higher, being or insight.

At first, I was struck with grief, caused by the dawning realization that all development is based on death, even though, as we will see, this 'death' is an illusion. For the growing consciousness of a human being, the physical body has to die.

For a butterfly to be born, its earlier stages have to die. For Christ to grow, John the Baptist had to diminish. And, for a higher development in the spiritual world, the old gods have to die in order for new ones to take over.

And now, this entity that I had grown fond of, the one that called himself Vidar, 'died' right in front of my eyes so that an even brighter being could appear. Why did it have to be that way? This is still a mystery I have difficulty to accept or understand, although deep down in my soul I think I can do both.

So, now I am standing there, with this bright entity in front of me, and the cracked body of Vidar lying on the ground but still looking at me, with one eye open, his right. He looked just like his deceased father, Odin.

As days passed during this increasingly overwhelming experience of the apparently dying Vidar and the gradual appearance of the new entity, several details became conscious to my soul. (It was no coincidence that all this – actually my entire travel through the tunnel, the three elemental realms and the etheric worlds – occurred in close connection to the fireplace. For in this fire, where 'living' wood dies or is destroyed, a spiritual existence is easier to observe.)

One morning, sitting before the flames, I experienced the following. Suddenly, several spiritual beings appeared within the flames, revealing the depths of 'their' spiritual world, which was somehow related to – and not totally different from – the spiritual world revealed by the 'new' entity within or behind Vidar. This was the sundered Odin, who day by day recovered more and more, and all the time fixated me piercingly with his one – right – eye. This new 'world' revealed by the flame-entities amazed me greatly.

It may take years to establish a connection to the spiritual world, but when this connection has once been established, it can be opened in a matter of seconds. Before, when I only knew the inner etheric world together with the third realm of the elemental world, I had seen the darker forces, the demonic world. I understood now that this demonic world was related to material creation, expressed in the wall of the tunnel, possibly also partly in the inner etheric world, the inside of the tunnel. But now, in the outside, everything was growing with abundant life: the trees, the plants and the dead. And the present and past revealed itself, much as in the way I have described concerning trees (in my Norwegian book, *Pappel*). These etheric streams between the trees seem to be an aspect of the life-giving 'outer' part of the etheric world – which was now revealed in all its glory with the help of Vidar and the entity that he was hiding. It seems that the outer etheric world is related to time, or that the opening of the outer etheric world opens or reveals the illusion of time bound to the inner etheric world.

Another effect of this outer etheric world being enlivened and 'visible', is that the realm of the dead became penetrable for my sight, as well as the etheric forces of the natural world.

I understand now that, earlier in life, I did have some access to this etheric world through my connection to trees, as described in the aforementioned book, *Pappel*. There, I described how I entered the living, etheric streams that connect all trees, and thus can enter time itself. When I stand in the path of such an etheric stream and go to the right, I enter the future. When I go to the left, I enter the past.

*

When viewing Vidar's sundered head and looking into his right eye, this indicated that he could open the path to the future. The entity that he now revealed when he fell apart, had only his left eye directed at me – or, more correctly, it was only the left eye that I could see. Thus, this entity allowed me to see into the past.

So, in this meeting with the double entity in the outer etheric realm, I could enter both future and the past: truly an Akashic opening! I also understand that both Vidar, Balder and Life itself are related to each other and to this outer etheric world, this world of cloudy existence, where it is possible to experience the glory of Life itself, and to meet Christ.

*

Now Spring was approaching, and the birds and insects were lively. The first green shoots on the trees became visible and life showed its unstoppable force. But still, the two entities remained distant and serious. I could find very little contact, recognition or joy in their faces. I tried to make them see me, contact me, be joyous, but in vain.

Then one evening something happened. Suddenly, a huge shell or veil fell off the entities' faces. It was like a constraining layer cracked open, and the two beings stepped out into the open, smiling brightly, warmly welcoming me into their radiant light.

I was astonished. All this time I had thought that I was seeing them, I had only been looking at a veil. Then I realized that most of what we think and see *is* veiled. Even the famous Isis of Egypt was veiled, and at her feet was an inscription that read: 'I am the past, the present and the future. No mortal shall lift my veil.' For our present time, Rudolf Steiner said that the inscription should read: '... every mortal *should* lift my veil ...'.

Why is this so? Why is the whole of creation covered by a veil, or even two or three? Probably because we are not ready to see reality, to see creation as it is, to see the face of spiritual beings and to see the face of God. In olden times, people believed that one who saw the face of God died immediately. Or, became insane.

After this experience, I began to see a certain movement, a certain image through the different veils that cover everything. All things are veiled. The birds, the trees and the whole of Creation as such. Everything we see is nothingness – just veils.

Then I received an inspiration:

- The inner etheric world is veiled by illusions of 'life'.
- The three elemental realms are veiled by illusions of 'strength'.
- The outer etheric world is veiled by illusions of 'love'.

These illusions cover up reality for our perception.

This deep realization of the multiple veils brought a profound confusion and sorrow, a deep frustration that was not yet able to be met by the ability to go deeper – to see a truer visage of the two entities who, until now, had been presented as Vidar and Balder. This frustration was due to the realization that we see so little of reality, and that most of what we see is illusion.

Rudolf Steiner went so far as to say that everything that has a name is 'nothing', and that all is 'I-consciousness', or simply the 'I'.

Without illusions, there would be no possibility of error, and subsequently no possibility for freedom and development of consciousness – and as a consequence, no possibility of free and spiritual love, which is the main goal of this Earth incarnation.

*

Rudolf Steiner stated that Christ descended/ascended into the etheric world with his etheric body at the beginning of the twentieth century. Christ can be found there. And if we are not able to find him there during the next 2,000 years, that would be devastating for the human race.

There is a threefold inclination towards the spiritual world in the human soul:

1. To know the divine behind the world.
2. To know Christ in His relation to human beings.
3. To know the spirit in its working in the world.

   - The denial of the divine is a physical sickness.
   - The denial of Christ is a calamity of the soul.
   - The denial of the spirit is a sign of defectiveness of the spirit.

My questions regarding this are as follows:

1. Can we find Christ in the physical world, which is purely *maya*?
2. Can we find Christ in the elemental world, the world created mainly by the adversarial forces?
3. Can we find Christ in the inner etheric world, the world where the 'uninitiated' souls of the dead travel?
4. Can we find Christ in the outer etheric world, the world that I described as 'cloud-filled', and where I met Vidar?
5. Can we go directly to the etheric world, without working through the physical and elemental worlds and realms?

Rudolf Steiner once said that to find the 'Father', we first had to go through the 'Holy Spirit', then through 'Christ'. Only then could we reach the Father.

Could this mean that we first go through the third realm, the realm of earthly structure, the inner area of the etheric, where we experience the 'Holy Spirit'? Then, the second realm, the planetary and atomic realm, the outer area of the etheric, where we would experience the 'Christ'; and then, the first realm, the cosmic vacuum, the conjunction of the two areas, where we would experience the 'Father'?

If it is so that the second realm of the elemental world opened in 1949, and the first realm in 2019, did that change our path to the etheric world and Christ, and was Rudolf Steiner aware of how these changes would affect our way into the spiritual world? Perhaps these future changes were to be discussed in Steiner's Second and Third Classes of his School of Spiritual Science?

*

During this period, I slowly understood that this changing of appearance was actually a part of a teaching. The spiritual entities taught me about illusions, and changed their appearance for this purpose – even pretending to be dead and disintegrating. Once I understood this, they became fully 'alive' again, and began a deeper conversation with me.

Every time they wanted or tried to teach me something, it was always preceded or accompanied with depression and confusion – also, with a total inability to play chess!

The next thing I was taught was the difference between dead thinking and living thinking. This concept had bothered me for many years, as I had difficulties in grasping the difference. I thought that all thinking was more or less alive – especially my own thinking, as I usually thought in moving pictures; moving and alive images. Again, this was of course an illusion and an error.

I was taught that life is always present in the process, and death in the finished product. So, even if I think about the finished product 'in moving pictures', my thinking is dead. If I think about the process itself, then I can observe, in moving pictures, the developing process behind the object. Then, I come to living thinking.

This was a bit like the observations I made in my book *Poplar*. I can observe the tree, even the etheric structure of the tree, but still the thinking is dead. If I then go into the etheric and 'turn left', I perceive the past. Still, the thinking is dead. If I 'turn right', I perceive the future – and as the future is not crystallized out into physical forms but is still in a process, then the thinking becomes alive.

After realizing this, my depression disappeared. Then, we – the two spiritual entities and myself – went into a sort of educational relationship in which they put me in situations that I had to understand and learn from. It was almost like a karmic education.

The next lesson came some days later, and this was a logical continuation from the previous one, based upon understanding illusion. It was also based upon my experiences at Stonehenge, several years before. After visiting Stonehenge several times, I came to the point where I stopped observing or concentrating on the stones themselves, but instead directed my observation to the spaces *between* the stones. There I found a living, spiritual reality, containing the knowledge of the old Druids, laid down for coming generations to discover.

So, after some days of observing the two entities of the outer etheric world, I followed their silent instructions to consider them, or at least their appearance, as *maya*, as illusion. I directed my spiritual gaze 'between' them, just as I had with the stones at Stonehenge, and the same happened. A whole world revealed itself behind the door or gate created by, or in, the space between the two entities – between Vidar and Balder.

It was as if these two entities were guardians of the threshold to the outer etheric world. They would not let me pass until I had realized the illusion of everything, even in the spiritual world.

I also had to realize that the world in which Christ lived had to be found between two entities, as the Christ emphasized that he would be found in the middle, between two or three that are gathered in his name* (we were myself, Vidar and Balder). It all made so very much sense now. Thus, I could travel further, 'behind' the two entities, with whom I had been occupied now for several weeks.

They had taken a step apart from each other, creating a sort of gateway between them, leading into this outer etheric world. My first impression of the world behind was of immense strength, a vast and overwhelming, benevolent power.

The month of May had arrived, and all was growing and thriving in outer nature. Likewise, I felt that my inner life was blossoming too, with the opening of the gate to the outer etheric world.

My encounter with Vidar, Balder and this outer etheric proceeded, one tiny step each earthly day – especially in the mornings, during my meditation in front of the fireplace.

The next step was when – having just crossed some sort of threshold between the two entities and looking back on them, watching the opening between them – I was able to see that they formed a gate, a portal. It was now clear that they formed a gate through which – two earthly days previously – I had passed.

One of the entities was huge and strong and glowed in bluish colours, whilst the other was smaller and glowed in reddish colours. As I now saw them from the other side, it was difficult to perceive which was Balder and which was Vidar, but I came to the conclusion that the big, bluish entity standing on the right (left when seen from my new situation, looking backwards) was Balder. The smaller, reddish entity, then, was Vidar.

One other interesting feature was that Vidar was standing on the bare and very dry – dryer than normal – rock, whilst Balder was standing on wet and swampy ground. Between them, they definitely made a portal… and a threshold. Could it be that, in this situation, in front of the outer etheric world, they were working as the guardians of this threshold?

*

---

* 'For where two or three gather in my name, there am I with them.' (Matthew 18:20.)

During the following days, the structures of this outer etheric world started to become slightly more present. It was not only clouds that were visible, but I also began to see other structures, all in different shades of grey. But more and more over the coming days, and more interestingly, these diffuse contours of grey crystallized out to resemble a series of huge mountains – like the Himalayas in Tibet or the Rila mountain range of Bulgaria.

This 'land' on the other side of Vidar and Balder seemed to consist of two areas: one huge flatland, like the tundra of Siberia, and one huge mountainous area. Vidar stood in front of the huge flatland, an area with grass and bushes.* In these flatlands, many rivers and lakes were present, as well as the waterfalls and rivers coming down from the mountains.

As such, three elements seem to constitute this vast land: the earth of the flatlands, the rocks of the mountains and the water of the rivers (in both the flatlands and the mountains). Thus, rock – water – earth.

In his book *Occult Science*, as well as in his *Theosophy*, Rudolf Seiner describes 'spirit land' as consisting of three areas that are characterized as 'solid', 'fluid' and 'aeriform'. Could it be somewhat the same here, only that I couldn't yet see it properly?

One thing made me a little sad. This land was completely bereft of astral inhabitants – only etheric life, such as plants, could be seen. Where was this astral life, I asked myself? Is there none because this is the etheric realm, where only plant-life 'lives'?

I had already previously travelled to the 'mountains' of the outer etheric world without being aware of it, as described in my book, *Poplar*. Here is a quotation from the final part of that book:

> *Slowly my consciousness ceases to work.*
> *The ray of light again gets stronger.*
> *The metallic smell of a different reality appears.*
> *I try to see.*
> *Memories of the spiritual world vibrate softly in my consciousness.*
> *All I ever loved, touches me like a spring breeze.*
> *All that is said or read is crystal clear in my consciousness.*
> *The night is falling, and the stars shine bright.*
> *All paths are telling me where they lead to.*
> *The dust disappears.*

---

* It is interesting to note that in the old Germanic mythology, Vidar (Widar) lived in 'Vide', meaning a wide flatland.

It feels like I come near to another world; the world where I once came from. To enter the network of the trees, their singing, black and waving weave, is somehow like entering death. After I have looked at, experienced, entered and lived with this living network for some years, I start to realize that the whole of it is an illusion.

I am in a deserted mountain landscape. There is no life. The rocks are barren and hard. I am walking there without knowing where I should go. Anyway, I am pulled up, upwards towards higher summits. The air gets thinner and I get exhausted. Anyway, I walk on and on.

I can see a cross in the distance. A black cross appears, standing alone in this deserted mountain landscape. Now I have a destination. It becomes easier to breathe, and I come closer and closer to the cross.

After a while I notice there is something in the crossing point... I get closer and see that this is a rosi-crucifix. It has seven or twelve roses, sometimes twenty-four roses, shaping a wreath around the crossing point. I get closer and closer, and soon I can differentiate the single roses.

The roses are stylized, they are immovable. Sitting there untouchable, fixed to a black crucifix in the endless mountain landscape. I look at them for many days, until I become exhausted.

In my exhaustion, I reach for the hand of my lover. I hold my lover's hand... and something miraculous happens. Everything becomes alive; the ground of the mountain begins to live and to move, as if it is turning into a plant, a wooden and living cover of wood.

Then the crucifix itself begins to change, gets brighter, starts to live and an eye appears, seeing me. The roses too become alive after a while, they grow, move, create bowls ... dripping nectar.

And I see that the whole energetic network of nature originates from this crucifix.

What is complete, intricate, karmic and all-embracing, has its origin here.

The circle is closed, and I lay down my pen, and at the same time life slowly starts to disappear...

*

After contemplating the lack of astral inhabitants for some two weeks, one morning I had a revelation. When I am living and travelling in the normal material world, I never see any spiritual beings, unless I cross the Northern threshold. In short, I have to 'fade' into nature in order to accomplish a loosening of the bond between the physical and the etheric. Then, I am able to see the spiritual inhabitants of the spiritual world, which I now call the 'inner' etheric world – the etheric world bound up to our material creation, the 'waters' that are under the firmament, as described in Genesis in the Bible.* Maybe this first procedure works the same in the outer etheric world, in the waters 'above' the firmament? What if I had to do this again, in the outer etheric world?

I repeated the passing of the threshold and tried to follow this decision. I 'faded' and travelled past the three elemental realms and ventured into the outer etheric world, way past the gate formed by Vidar and Balder. There I stopped and looked around. I saw an empty land, with the huge mountain range, the flatlands and all the rivers, as described earlier.

Then I repeated the procedure whilst being in the physical world, crossing the first threshold by fading into nature.

This time I faded into the nature of the outer etheric world.

What an amazing result! A huge quantity of beings and entities emerged forth... The land was suddenly populated! It was an experience equal to when I first crossed the threshold between the physical/material world and the third realm of the elemental world. Then I suddenly 'saw' the etheric creatures of this world, although I had first to meet and experience the demonic realm (as described in my book *Demons and Healing*).

In this outer etheric world, I did not meet demonic hosts, as I did when entering the elemental realms and the inner etheric world; only spiritual beings of light. It was as if this outer etheric world had been cleansed of demons, and that they had gathered in the etheric world closest to the physical world in which we live – the etheric related closely to the three elemental realms.

---

* 'And God made the firmament, and divided the waters which were under the firmament from the waters which were above the firmament: and it was so. And God called the firmament Heaven. And the evening and the morning were the second day. And God said, Let the waters under the heaven be gathered together unto one place, and let the dry land appear: and it was so.' (Genesis 1: 7-8.)

In this new experience, everything was quite chaotic, at least during the first days. It seemed like all the entities that had their dwelling in this outer etheric world were intertwined – they were all together in a common experience of their reality. They were all living together in the light of God, or at least this was how I experienced it initially. It also seemed to me that the entities of this region showed a certain joy and happiness concerning my 'arrival' – that I was suddenly able to 'see' them. In a way, they 'frolicked', in both the mountains and over the land. The medium through which they moved was partly clouds and partly light-filled air. I couldn't do other than observe this joy.

Days passed, and I could begin to witness a certain hierarchy among the inhabiting entities. There was a certain difference in rank, in importance, as well as to where the different entities 'belonged'. The most interesting for me, though, was that no demonic influence could be detected. It seems that all demonic entities are to be found in the inner etheric realm or in the three elemental realms, and that there are none outside of this.

I was now ready to travel and investigate this outer etheric world. This research will almost certainly continue for the rest of my life, so I will have to publish this book before it comes to an end, as it never will! It is a never-ending story…

After patiently watching the frolicking entities of this realm for some time, I decided to do something active in order to investigate further. I tried to change focus, just as one does in a microscope, or with a pair of binoculars. When the focus is changed, one sees quite differently. I focused in closer, and there emerged a huge house with three sections. The section to the left was the past, the one to the right was the future and the one in the middle was the present.

I enlarged my focus to include the mountains. Then a huge tower emerged – a tower with many floors – reaching very high up, although I could see the spire at the top. I could not decide how many floors there were… maybe ten to fifteen?

So, I could now change my focus, and thus was revealed that this vast land consisted of three realities – realities that existed in different depths and also in different directions. There was:

- the house close by, stretching out from left to right, relating to the passing of time;

- the living and weaving area between, stretching out from me and far away, relating to a sort of celebration of life;
- and the tower at the back, stretching from below to above, relating to the development of consciousness, or one might say the different hierarchies of Angels.

Each of these realities were further divided in a certain number of sections. I only could guess what these were.

- When I ventured more closely into the 'house', I experienced a differentiation of my own soul forces, so that *will* was emphasized, then thinking, then feeling.
- In the 'flatlands' the experience was that *feeling* was emphasized, then will, then thinking.
- In the 'tower' it was as if *thinking* was emphasized, then feeling, then will.

And in the middle of it all, like an all-encompassing light, warm, pleasant and all-loving, I felt the presence of Christ; not as a person and not in any earthly form, but as a presence – a consciousness.

I always thought that my meeting with Christ would be like meeting a person. But it was not like that at all. It was an experience *of and with* the Light of the World, a personal, all-encompassing, all-penetrating and all-seeing *Light*.

In the following days I felt as if I was penetrated by this light.

*

After some days, my curious, investigative mind started to research and experiment with this shining and penetrating Light. Up until then, I had received the light, this Godly Light, this Christ Sun, with my head, with my eyes and with my third eye. To these parts or areas of my being, the light was 'just' light, although filled with love and grace, kindness and understanding. One morning, however, I tried to receive the light with my heart, and its character and presence changed radically.

A compassionate face appeared within the light. As the strength of the light diminished, the face appeared. Then I lowered my consciousness further down, to the pelvic area, and the shining light revealed a strong power – a will that seemed to be totally absent in the shining light received by the area of the head. Three ways, or maybe a continuum, of receiving this Christ force.

Does this mean that Christ may be within us, activating our whole body, our thinking, feeling and will? 'It is no longer I who live, but Christ who lives in me', were the words that Paul uttered.* Did he feel or experience the same?

At this point, I will add a very personal comment on my bodily wellbeing. As mentioned, since March 2020 I had suffered heavily with the after-effects of Covid-19. I was without energy, unable to do physical work, endured constant headaches for long periods, suffered from poor sleep, and also experienced other symptoms of fatigue.

When I entered the outer etheric realm, all these problems quickly disappeared. I felt that my strength reappeared, my sleep got better and my ability to travel, talk and walk returned. This development accelerated markedly when I 'found' the shining light, the Christ sun, of the outer etheric realm.

There is a verse by Rudolf Steiner that I say every morning:

> *Godly light*
> *Christ sun,*
> *Warm our hearts,*
> *Enlighten our heads,*
> *That good may become,*
> *What we from hearts found,*
> *What we from heads direct with single will†*

This would suggest that the experience and reception of Christ differs in relation to whether He is received through the head or through the heart.

As a personal experience, I would like to add the possibility for Christ to be received through our will-system, our limbs and digestive system. Thus:

> *.... so that good may become,*
> *What we from hearts found,*
> *What we from heads direct with single will*
> **What we through our limbs' action cause in the world.**

*

---

* 'I have been crucified with Christ. It is no longer I who live, but Christ who lives in me.' (Galations 2:20.)

† Drawn from Rudolf Steiner's 'Foundation Stone Meditation'.

This Godly light is the foundation of all physical matter, as love is the foundation of our whole being of soul. Matter is condensed Light, and our soul is condensed Love. Love and light, streaming out from the Christ being, are thus the foundation of all.

In this situation, I thought, it is of crucial importance to differentiate between the divine Light and Lucifer's light within the light; likewise, between the divine will and Ahriman's will in the limbs and earthly substances; as well as between the brotherly face of Christ in the heart and the coming powers of the Azuras, which will also appear close to the heart.

Another question I asked myself at this stage was as follows: If I become aware of the Christ light, which is the foundation of matter, will I be able to become aware of the light within matter? Will matter start to 'shine'? Likewise, if I become aware of the Christ-will in the limbs... and Christ's face within the heart... Again, will I then be able to say 'Christ in me'...?

But it was not that simple, of course. The adversarial forces did not allow such a simple procedure to succeed. We have to be hindered and tested... And, being in a physical/material body has to imply the presence of the adversarial forces. So, how could I combine both?

During the days of struggling with these questions, we were enjoying wonderful Spring weather. But despite the growing and blossoming around me, my practical and logical abilities were almost completely absent. I could not think clearly in the physical/material world, although the 'logic' of the etheric world flowed freely.

In a way, this logic was the same, but also very different. It was as if a moral intuition had entered into mathematical and physical considerations. That depressed me, as I found it so difficult to comprehend.

One thing I thought about much, and that made me wonder, was why the 'face of Christ', which I saw with my heart, was not a conventionally 'beautiful' face. The spirit and light of Christ, which I saw with my eyes, or head region, was utterly beautiful. The 'will of Christ', which I saw from my pelvic area, appeared strong and attractive. And the 'face of Christ', seen from my heart region, was full of compassion and love – although the form was somewhat

unusual.* It was not symmetrical, as we humans usually define a
beautiful face. Much research has been done on what makes a face

---

* When I say that I see something or someone through the 'head region' or
'through the heart', this needs some explanation. The first time I became
aware of this possibility was when I read the books of Carlos Castaneda. He
elaborates what his guru, an Indian shaman called Don Juan, explains about
going into different realities. The technique he used was to move what he
called 'the Assemblage Point' to different places in the body. By doing this,
he reached different realities, sometimes *totally* different ones.

When I trained the 'Northern way of passing the threshold', I developed a
certain ability to consciously divide the different bodies, the physical, etheric
and astral bodies. I also experimented in moving my consciousness – this
factor that I think Castaneda talked about – probably a composition of the
conscious part of the 'I' (part of the future cosmic 'I'), the conscious part of
the astral body (part of the future Manas), the conscious part of the etheric
body (part of the future Buddhi) and maybe a small part of the conscious
physical body (part of the future Atma).

Up through the years, I have moved this 'package' around in my body and
have then observed the world around me, the physical, etheric and astral
worlds, even the spiritual or elemental beings that I could see. Doing this,
I observed that the different parts or beings changed quite a lot. They thus
revealed totally different aspects of their own being.

I experimented in watching through my twelve sense organs, through
my seven organs and through my thinking, feeling or will. When I thus
observed the inner etheric realm, the one inside the tunnel, I perceived it
through the *thinking* as shining light (as some modern humans experience
the after-death travel through the tunnel), through the *feeling* as a river of
crystal clear water (called Styx, as the Greeks experienced the after-death
travel through the tunnel, led by the ferryman Karon) or through the *will*
as a walk through a very dry desert (as the later Greeks experienced the
after-death travel through the tunnel, as a void landscape).

When with this method I observe the Christ, His appearance changes quite
a lot. Through *thinking*, the appearance is as divine light, through *feeling* as
a somewhat unattractive ever-changing face, and through *will* as divine
creation, as divine will.

Through the three sacrifices of the Nathan soul, the Christ being has all knowledge of the human being: the twelve sense organs from Lemurian times, the seven
organs from early Atlantean times, the thinking/feeling/will from late Atlantean
times, and of course the whole body and collected knowledge from the Golgotha
sacrifice at the turning point of time. With this background, the Christ being will
be perceived very differently according to from *where* he is observed.

look attractive to human beings, and regularity and symmetry are usually important factors.

Now, I must add that I personally have always found a certain irregularity more attractive. I find irregularity in the eyes, for example, utterly beautiful. Likewise with teeth – I find a certain irregularity to be attractive.

In the face of Christ, I found much irregularity – too much to be beautiful in a conventional, 'human' sense. The lower face was too forceful, and the line of the mouth was not even – the left part was lower than the right. In this context, I think of the face of Christ as Rudolf Steiner modelled it in his wooden sculpture. It is also quite irregular, and not conventionally 'beautiful'. I would expect that Jesus, the man, was immensely beautiful. However, presumably the Christ spirit would not be characterized by earthly concepts of beauty. Perhaps this is the explanation.

Rudolf Steiner's artistic depiction of Christ

*

One evening in May this year (2021), there was a heavy thunderstorm. The lightning was fierce and frequent. As I now live virtually always in the vicinity of the Christ Light, I also observed this light during the storm. It changed in a very peculiar way. The light transformed from what I have described as a calm and soothing, loving light to a 'sharper' form. It was as if the lightning sharpened the light in some mysterious way. It became more 'wilful', if I can describe it so.

After this experience, I became more and more able to see this shining light in all of nature. Of course, I did not see this light with my physical eyes, but with my spiritual eyes. More and more, I could see that everything glowed with the same light as was emitted from the Christ being in the outer etheric realm.

The phrase 'Not I, but Christ in me' – or better, 'Not I, but Christ in my "I"' – increasingly, in addition, became: 'Not I, but Christ in all'.

This situation remained, as described, for a long time.

*

I lived in the 'normal' world, but visited both the inner etheric region as well as the three elemental realms as often as I wanted and could. But mostly my interest and observations stayed with the outer etheric world, as this was so beautiful, light-filled and powerful. Besides, I had investigated the inner etheric, together with the third elemental realm, for so many years that it really did not interest me that much anymore. It is important to understand that when one has first been in a certain part of the spiritual worlds, it is very easy to visit this area again – even if it had taken one many years to get there the first time. It is like having read a huge encyclopedia of many volumes. It takes years to read it all, but after having read it, it takes just a few seconds to look up the different subject areas to re-read or re-check what is written there. A crucial difference between the spiritual world and an encyclopedia, of course, is that each time one visits the spiritual world, it is slightly changed, or rather, that area has developed further. One could even say that every area in the spiritual world is multilayered so that one reaches a somewhat deeper layer each time one visits. In addition, every visit changes one a little, so that this change also leads to a different perception of the area in question. So, even if for some time I 'stood still' in my investigations, what I had already discovered continued to develop at its own pace.

*

A very good friend of mine asked me to ask Vidar what he wanted us to do in today's world, in order to clear the way for the coming of Christ. So, I went back to the gate of the 'outer' etheric world and tried to communicate with Vidar.

As he is part of the 'post-*Ragnarök*' world – the world where the new spirituality is supposed to grow and develop, and where Balder will become alive again with the new clairvoyance – I tried to ask

Vidar where I should put my effort in order to help in this development. It took some time before he answered. Then, he looked down to his right, at an angle of about 45 degrees, and his gaze penetrated the superficial layer of the earth beneath him. I followed his sharp gaze, and could see where it stopped, where it concentrated its attention. It stopped at a lump of dark soil. This soil was special – it was dense and full of shining life, with a certain amount of crystalline graphite. His Christ-filled glittering gaze was directed straight into this area of earth. He filled it with Christ-penetrated life.

The lump of earth could also be seen as consisting of shining black coal, representing both the etheric and life-giving earth, and also the stone of wisdom, the so-called 'Philosopher's Stone'. After some time I think I understood. I will try and touch on the truth of this in the following passages.

*

Rudolf Steiner stated very clearly that humanity could not reach its goal of achieving the new clairvoyance of the post-*Ragnarök* period without a nutrition that was filled with etheric substance. Dr Ehrenfried Pfeiffer* wrote of this as follows:

> This can be understood against the background of a conversation I had with Dr Steiner on route from Stuttgart to Dornach shortly before the agricultural course was given. He had been speaking of the need for a deepening of esoteric life, and in this connection mentioned certain faults typically found in spiritual movements. I then asked, 'How can it happen that the spiritual impulse, and especially the inner schooling, for which you are constantly providing stimulus and guidance, bear so little fruit? Why do the people concerned give so little evidence of spiritual experience, in spite of all their efforts? Why, worst of all, is the will for action, for the carrying out of these spiritual impulses, so weak?' I was particularly anxious to get an answer to the question as to how one could build a bridge to active participation and the carrying out of

---

* Ehrenfried Pfeiffer (1899–1961) was a German scientist, soil scientist, leading advocate of biodynamic agriculture, anthroposophist and student of Rudolf Steiner.

spiritual intentions without being pulled off the right path by personal ambition, illusions and petty jealousies; for, these were the negative qualities Rudolf Steiner had named as the main inner hindrances. Then came the thought-provoking and surprising answer: 'This is a problem of nutrition. Nutrition as it is today does not supply the strength necessary for manifesting the spirit in physical life. A bridge can no longer be built from thinking to will and action. Food plants no longer contain the forces people need for this.[*]

That is why Rudolf Steiner gave an extensive course on how to grow food. This agricultural course was held from 7 to 16 June 1924, in the home of Count and Countess Keyserlingk, at Koberwitz near Breslau. It was followed by further consultations and lectures, among them Steiner's well-known 'Address to Youth'.[†]

So far so good. But then I discovered a book written by Paul Emberson with the title *The Death of Nutrition*.[‡] He adds some crucial information, obtained from memoirs from Countess Keyserlingk as well as her son, Adalbert, who was only 19-years-old at the time of Steiner's agricultural course, and was admitted to a special 'esoteric lesson' on Whit Sunday. This meeting had not been publicized and no notes were taken, so few are even aware that it occurred.

The main agricultural course was delivered to farmers and scientists, but only a few of these, perhaps a handful, gathered at this lesson, after the main course had taken place, in order to participate within this chosen group – chosen principally for their potential to experience the living Christ in the etheric.[§]

Emberson describes that Steiner explained to this group that the methods and results of the main course were, on their own, not

---

[*] From Preface to Rudolf Steiner, *Agriculture Course*, p. 7, Rudolf Steiner Press 2004.

[†] See *Youth and the Etheric Heart*, SteinerBooks 2007.

[‡] Published by The DewCross Centre for Moral Technology 2019.

[§] In *Birth of a New Agriculture* (Temple Lodge 1999), Countess Keyserlingk writes: 'In addition to the two addresses to the young members on 9 and 17 June, and two Class lessons, Rudolf Steiner held an esoteric lesson on Whit Sunday, during the Agricultural Course, after a walk through the park and the garden. There is hardly anyone who remembers it.'

enough to give plants sufficiently strong, clean etheric forces to support humanity's spiritual development and striving. This could only be obtained by incorporating the Christ forces into the methods, preparations and work of the farmers. Emberson's book, with its stark conclusions, made a deep impression on me.

Now, following the gaze of Vidar, I suddenly understood his message – and also Steiner's intentions and insights – and why he did not tell these secrets to the participants on the main course. My own conclusions and insights from Vidar´s gaze were as follows:

- The etheric forces, present in earthly creation today, are mainly derived from the 'inner' etheric world. They are too strongly influenced by the adversarial forces in order to be able to raise human consciousness sufficiently.
- We must draw etheric forces from the 'outer' etheric world, where the Christ light is able to penetrate.
- Rudolf Steiner could not speak openly of this because this outer world was not then accessible to the bulk of humanity, as all three elemental realms had yet to be fully opened (in 1879, 1949 and 2019). Thus, the only way today is through the elemental world – to reach the threshold and gate of Vidar and Balder and the Christ Light, and with this light to penetrate the earth of growing plants to give sufficient etheric energy to humanity, enabling human beings to reach the future consciousness of Jupiter and Christ.
- By incorporating the Christ etheric into the earth, especially into the growing of nutritional plants, we also activate the Philosopher's Stone.

This moment of communication, although it was only through the eyes, seems to have been a turning point in my relationship to the gatekeepers of the 'outer' etheric world. It seems that this communication made the guardian more aware of me, and, from that moment, he seemed to see me in a more personal way. After that, he began to communicate more directly with me, not only through the eyes or the intellect, but straight to my heart. From his heart to my heart.

*

The next day, this dark, shining, graphite-like earth grew in my mind. I saw it as a living image the whole time. It demanded an answer – it demanded me to understand its existence. I thought I understood what it meant when I made a connection to the living, Christ-imbued earth, but there was something more – something important, which I strived to understand or 'see'.

After some time, Vidar's communication continued. He indicated that this connection to the Christ-light and the outer etheric realm relating to farmers, also referred to doctors and teachers – actually to all kinds of workers, but first and foremost to farmers, doctors and teachers.

After this initial communication with Vidar, which at first was only an indicative look of his eyes, a certain 'non-verbal' teaching began. He urged me, by the indicative look he sent, to take a closer look at the dark, shining, graphite-like earth. After some time, I could see that within this earth, within this Philosopher's Stone, there was an eye. Vidar let me understand that this eye was actually the other eye of Odin, and this was the foundation of his relation-ship, or companionship, with Balder. Odin had placed this eye into the well of Mimer* – a passageway between the outer and the inner etheric realms – in exchange for wisdom; wisdom of 'Middle-earth'.

I did not grasp this at first. Then, Vidar indicated that in ancient times there was full communication between the gods and humans. With the coming of the Dark Age, Kali Yuga, this communication slowly got lost, being hindered by the materiality of Creation. This resulted in the wall of the 'tunnel', as described earlier. The outer etheric world, where the gods lived, was firmly separated by the inner world of the etheric, which was of course needed for life to endure on earth. Odin, the Archangel, then placed his one eye in the inner world of the etheric, so that he could still communicate with human beings, and thus receive wisdom and insight into the life of humans. The Edda tells that Odin could even walk on the material (human) earth.

This 'wall' consisted of three realms, one dominated by the lucif-eric beings, one by the ahrimanic beings and the last by the azuric beings. When Kali Yuga ended in 1879, the third, 'luciferic', realm was opened, and a certain communication between the human world, the inner etheric realm and the outer etheric realm could

---

* Mímir or Mim is a figure in Norse mythology, renowned for his knowledge and wisdom, who is beheaded during the Æsir-Vanir War. Afterwards, the god Odin carries around Mímir's head and it recites secret knowledge and counsel to him.

begin. In 2019, the opening was total, and Odin/Balder could then fully connect with the 'earthly eye' – in a way to 'claim his eye' – and a new clairvoyance could start to develop among humans on earth.

This 'eye of communication' with the gods remains on the earth, and this communication can bring divine forces into the earth, but only when mediated by human beings that are in connection with the outer etheric realm, that is, with the Light of the Christ. Only when farmers have this connection, and use the spiritual preparations of biodynamic agriculture, can they bring enough divine forces into human nourishment, and thus make possible the developing new 'Christ-related' clairvoyance.

*

Another thing occurred one morning. Vidar stopped his indicative use of glances, but started to 'talk' to me in a human way. At first, the language was impossible to understand – it was totally foreign. I had no idea what he said. Additionally, he sent his stream of words away from me – and again, I did not understand this. I tried to understand him using several different means, but all in vain. Then I got the idea of 'transforming' the language to a language I could understand. I got the idea for this 'transformation' through visiting the old megalithic site in Tanum near Tanumshede in Sweden. There, I had observed an interesting method that the ancients had used to understand the cosmic language of the zodiac. They mirrored the cosmic 'rays', the incoming zodiacal information, by the help of a huge – about twenty-metres-long – stone that reflected and centred the incoming rays to a certain focal point. This is almost the same principle used today in TV parabolas (satellite dishes). Then, the initiate could stand or sit in the focal-point and receive insights. Such mirrored and centred light has been used for millennia as a means to get information. I have seen similar phenomena described by the Native Americans, the Roma (Gypsies) – whose use of a crystal bowl can reflect and focus the incoming light in an ingenious way – as well as old European initiates, such as Jacob Böhme.

I tried to use this technique with the language of Vidar. I reflected the stream of words in a mental concave mirror, and let the stream go straight back towards my head – actually to my left ear. The language changed from a continuous stream of incomprehensible words to a language I could recognize. I could distinguish the words from one another, but still I could not understand what was being said. I had to continue to experiment with different angles and distances of this mirroring, reflecting and bending of his words – also receiving them through my ears, through my head or through my heart. All these ways gave a different clarity, a different percept, creating different concepts of what was said. It was like I was creating a method of translating one language to another – a foreign language to a known language. Thus, we went from:

1. indicative looks; to
2. non-verbal communication; to
3. a 'foreign' language; to
4. an incomprehensible language; to
5. a comprehensible language (at least to some degree).

This process took me several days of work. And I should remind my honoured reader that the words of a god may seem like folly to man – just as the words of a man may sound like folly to the gods.

*

Then something unexpected happened – something that has a long history. I should start at the beginning by describing my relationship to spiritual science and my ability to speak – or, my sense of language and sense of speech. Speech is of course one of the twelve senses that Rudolf Steiner describes, and this particular sense is a very spiritual one. It is about communication between two spiritual beings. It is also about the Creation of the world, for (as we know from the Gospel of St John): 'In the beginning was the Word…'.*

Three times in my life, my ability to speak and understand what is spoken has been radically altered. This occurred in conjunction with the alteration of the spiritual anatomy of my speech-sense organ. It seems to me that when the spiritual ability, or the spiritual anatomy of a sense-organ, or other spiritual constructions are altered, the physical ability to use the equivalent organ is changed or altered – or is even destroyed for some time.

---

* In the beginning was the Word, and the Word was with God, and the Word was God. He was in the beginning with God. All things were created through Him, and without Him nothing was created that was created. In Him was life, and the life was the light of mankind. The light shines in darkness, but the darkness has not overcome it. (John 1:1-5.)

The first time this happened was just after I had found the teachings of Rudolf Steiner for the first time, back in 1974. Then, suddenly, I totally lost all understanding of language. I could not understand anybody. This lasted for several hours. This experience changed the structure of my word-sense somewhat, so that I could now understand the spirituality behind the words of Steiner's books and lectures.

The second time this happened was many years later, just after I had been able to penetrate the deeper realms of the elemental world, in the spring of 2020. Then, suddenly, I became unable to speak or express myself, and again this lasted for several hours. This also changed my word-sense, so that I could express the spiritual intention behind the words I wanted to utter.

The third time this happened was just after I had met the guardian of the outer etheric world, the entity that had presented himself as Vidar, in the spring of 2021. Suddenly, I became unable to experience speech as a coherent stream. All sentences, all understanding and even my thinking, became divided in short and alternating periods of ability and non-ability, so that for five seconds I could speak and understand, and then for five seconds I could not, alternating all the time. This lasted for six hours. Also, my sight was influenced. When I could speak, I could focus, but when I could not speak, all was blurry. How this will alter or change my communication with Vidar, I do not yet know.

The important and interesting development after each such instance was that I had to reconquer the ability again afterwards – that is, to insert my will and consciousness into the ability. A spiritual change in the ability of perception seems thus to change the anatomy of the organ of physical perception, that is, the brain and the sense-organs, so that they may 'fit' each other.

The three levels of change that I have experienced up till now are as follows:

1. Inability to understand speech and activate clear thinking (1974).
2. Inability to speak, with half-clear thinking (2020).
3. Speech and thinking became sequenced, as total inability of both alternated with ability (2021).

Then, my understanding of what Vidar said became somewhat clearer. After this, he turned his eyes towards me. They were very soft, wise and full of will-power. A certain 'education' was directed in my direction, and it started by a stream of warmth – a stream going out from his eyes. And the eyes became more and more giving...

*

Vidar´s first direct teaching was, in a way, already demonstrated in his appearance at the threshold together with Balder. He taught me that all spiritual beings usually appear in couples. The two thus create a passage between them. It is through this passage that they communicate, appear or work. When one thus looks at an Angel – which, then, is usually a pair of Angels – they appear as two asymmetrical centres of force, streaming together in an outgoing stream between them. This gives the impression of an entity with two wings. In most appearances of spiritual beings described in the Bible, they are described as two entities working, walking or speaking in synchronicity. This new insight in the secret of the 'double' presence of spiritual beings triggered a huge change in my observation of both the spiritual world and of spiritual beings.

After this revelation it became much easier to 'see' spiritual beings.

*

For some weeks, Vidar appeared calm. It was as if he had told me what I needed to hear, and now he was resting. But one day his appearance changed again. From his initial childlike visage, to the apparent cracking up of his features (and resembling Odin), he now appeared as an Indian god. He continued to look down at me from somewhere above my head, on my right side. He had become silent again, simply watching me, quietly and calmly. This Indian god now streamed etheric consciousness, out of the foundations of Indian culture, for a whole week, from Sunday until the following Sunday. It was as if he became totally disconnected from the laws of the material world – from, as I was to understood, the mathematics of physical creation.

Then, on the Monday, Vidar's appearance changed, becoming somewhat Persian (Iranian), and it was as if he became much more interested in the world again, in the earth. By Wednesday, which coincided with Norway's 'opening', after the Covid-19 restrictions,*

---

* This indicated to me that there is a relationship between my spiritual journey towards Vidar and the Covid-19 pandemic.

Vidar's new appearance revealed to me that the whole of creation is based on mathematics. I saw mathematics in the straight lines of sunlight, in the 'speed' of sunlight, and in the construction of plants.

Then an unexpected teaching started to take form – the teaching of the change of rhythms in time. As a first example, Vidar used the seven days of the week. It took me some time to understand this teaching. This related in particular to the concept of God 'resting' on the seventh day.

As we know, the days of the week are related to the seven planets:

1. Sunday relates to the Sun.
2. Monday relates to the Moon.
3. Tuesday relates to Mars.
4. Wednesday relates to Mercury.
5. Thursday relates to Jupiter.
6. Friday relates to Venus.
7. Saturday relates to Saturn.

So, when does God rest? According to Vidar's teaching, the 'rest' comes as a quiet day, outside the seven-day cycle, and relates to God's consciousness, lingering in the outer etheric realm. In this way, the whole cycle becomes somewhat asymmetrical in the spiritual world, and time itself becomes dynamic.

I accept that these are very difficult concepts – difficult for me to interpret, difficult to articulate and difficult for others to comprehend. Nevertheless, I will try and put them into words:

After Saturday there is a rest, a period with quietness in the spiritual world. This quiet period, this rest, coincides with Sunday on the earthly material plane. However, after the quiet period comes the spiritual Sunday. This means that, in the second cycle, the spiritual Sunday falls on the earthly Monday. In turn, this means that Monday will be the day of the Moon, but with the superimposed (spiritual) aspect of Sunday.

In the next and third round, it is Tuesday that will carry the superimposed aspect of Sunday. This goes on, and on the eighth's cycle the spiritual aspect of Sunday will again be on a Sunday. This gives a cycle of eight, superimposed on a cycle of seven. In this way, Creation always changes and always offers something new.

I must say that I do not yet grasp the deeper consequences of this concept. I did understand, though, that the regular rhythm was dominant in the inner etheric realm and in the elemental world, but the rhythm was somewhat broken up in the outer etheric realm – stretched out in time – so that the earthly middle was not in the celestial middle. Perhaps like the golden ratio.

Soon after, on the following Tuesday, Vidar's Persian appearance changed dramatically to an Egyptian one. At this point, I understood that Vidar's teachings were neither perceptual nor conceptual at all, or even verbal. It was like a constant streaming of etheric understanding, which is almost impossible to put into words. (At the present time, it is actually impossible for me to explain this properly to myself, or even fully to conceptualize it within my own mind.)

The morning after this insight the teachings reached a definite climax. That was Friday morning, the fourth day of the Egyptian teaching. I had been up at 4.20 am to greet the rising sun, then had returned to bed and slept until 7.30 am. I went down to my fireplace and made a small fire. My morning conversation with Vidar then began.

He continued to focus on Egyptian culture and its strength. The 'teachings' were etheric in form, and were also strong – reaching an almost frightening power. It became increasingly clear to me that these kind of teachings were completely new, at least to myself. They streamed into my heart region – like a flowing river, like an avalanche...

*

After the Great War, Steiner reduced his engagements within Germany itself and started to operate and lecture increasingly in other countries (especially, of course, at the Goetheanum in Dornach, Switzerland). But he had a particular attraction to Great Britain, as witnessed in Crispian Villeneuve's two-volume work, *Rudolf Steiner in Britain.** How I interpret this interest is that Steiner started to change his presentations from the more intellectual, Central European 'I'-understanding to the etherically-influenced approach, i.e. from 'head-understanding' to 'heart-understanding'. This, too, is how I now experienced Vidar's teachings.

At the same time as these occurrences, I was reading Steiner's *Philosophy of Freedom*, where it is important to understand the difference between 'concept' and 'percept'. It became very clear to me what a difference there is between *conceptual* understanding and *etheric* understanding, and I really had to push my way through the

---

* Temple Lodge Publishing, 2009.

three elemental realms in order to reach a full etheric understanding. What I have called the 'Nordic way' of initiation (the Northern path) leads directly through the etheric element, through the inner etheric realm, through the three elemental realms and then the outer etheric realm or world, where Christ may be found.

*

Vidar's teachings continued later that day, coloured now by his Egyptian aura. These teachings were about life and death – particularly the mystery of death. Vidar led me to understand that death was actually equal to spiritual life, and that the mystery of death was incomprehensible to the adversarial forces, especially to Ahriman. Ahriman wanted to bring health, prosperity and good fortune in terms of a long (even eternal) life to the human being, and as such to avoid humanity finding the Christ or true spirituality.

Ahriman wanted modern medicine, modern vaccines and modern therapy to be effective and to prolong life beyond the allowances of karma (destiny). However, the 'good' forces of the spiritual world enable these things ultimately to fail. So, what appears to be good to the human being is actually bad, and vice versa.

While presenting me with this teaching on the mystery of death, Vidar grew to extraordinary proportions. He appeared extremely strong. The Indian god's presentation had appeared somewhat feminine and fragile and the Persian god's as intellectual and questioning, but the Egyptian god presented with an abundant power, muscular strength and an overwhelming will.

Just an hour later, Vidar seemed to have made his point, and went back to his 'normal' strength. This was on the Saturday of the third week, which means that – according to our description earlier – earthly Saturn's day was shone through by spiritual Jupiter.

The day after, on Sunday, Vidar's visage appeared again to 'crack', just like old porcelain – fragile and fissured. There was no teaching to be had on this day – or, maybe, his destruction *was* the teaching.

The next day (on the earthly) Monday, the body and face of this Egyptian god had cracked further, somewhat like porous limestone or decaying coral. Nothing further happened on that day.

Then Wednesday came, and the Imagination of Vidar stood there, directly in front of me, totally renewed as a Greek god, like Zeus – strong and full of mystery and magic. He just looked at me. He did not say anything and did not do anything.

On Saturday he started to teach again, and this took place much earlier than normal. He woke me up at the fourth hour of the fourth day of the 'Greek period' (of 8 days) which also is the fourth period, i.e. 4-4-4. He first showed me how the main characteristics of the form of Zeus are the balance between health and disease, and that the whole purpose of the Greek culture of 2,160* years was to unravel, and to understand the mystery of disease and sickness.

Vidar then gave a brief résumé of the previous cultures. The purpose of the first – Indian – culture was to understand the mystery of materiality. The second, the Persian, was to understand the mystery of nutrition; and the third – the Egyptian – was to understand the mystery of life and death. The real understanding of these mysteries was that, left to themselves, they would end up in destruction. The only force of salvation is the Christ force or Christ consciousness, which has to emerge in order to avoid this disastrous conclusion.

The above backs up Paul Emberson's claims in reference to Rudolf Steiner's agricultural course, i.e. that nutrition within food will not be sufficient without farmers being able consciously to bring in the Christ force. Likewise, I know from my medical practice that treatment without Christ consciousness will result in a 'translocation' of disease.[†] After these teachings had been received, it seems that a 'rest period' of sorts took place in the spiritual world.

The following day I was pondering why Vidar's initial teachings were about the cultural ages or epochs of humanity, but then I remembered that this was also the case with Rudolf Steiner, who often began his lectures with a shorter or longer recapitulation of the cultural ages of humanity. Thus, such understanding must be significant.

I await future teachings from Vidar.[‡] In the meantime I relate the above in all humility, in the hope that it will convey something of my 'travels' beyond the elemental realms.

---

* Plus possibly an additional seventh-part, that is 308 years, which represents a certain 'rest' between the cultures, but will result in a 'delay' in the destined cycle, so that the real length of the cycle would be 2,468 years.

[†] See further in my book *Spiritual Translocation*, Temple Lodge 2020.

[‡] These continue here in this book, in the postscript on p. 93.

Chapter 2

Seeing the Elemental Realms

Seeing into the first realm of the elemental world

In the first realm, we leave the structure of things, even the molecular or atomic structure, and are left with the streaming forces of vacuum, of the cosmos. To explain this I will describe the different levels at which one can perceive birds. When I look at a *crow* flying in the air, I see:

1. the material crow; then (going deeper),
2. the energetic streams in the body (etheric energy-streams). Then (going deeper),
3. the elemental being of the third realm, connected to and sustaining the crow, looking like a moving and ever-changing head of a wolf. Then (going deeper),
4. the elemental being(s) of the second realm, which looks like the (atomic) structure of iron. (Relating to the Archangelic realm of the third angelic hierarchy.) Then (going deeper),
5. the huge planet of Mars appears, pointing to the second hierarchy of the spiritual world (Dynamis realm of the second angelic hierarchy). Then (going deeper),
6. the elemental being(s) of the first realm appear, which as a structured entity cannot be observed, but the enormous power and movements of the cosmos reveal themselves as powerful underwater streams. This relates to the realm of the Archai of the third angelic hierarchy, which again relates to the first angelic hierarchy.

Looking at a *seagull*, the head of a horse appears in the third realm, the metal of silver as well as the planet of the Moon in the second realm, and the vast forces of the cosmos in the first realm.

Looking at a *hawk*, the head of an otter appears in the third realm, the metal of copper as well as the planet of Venus in the second realm, and again the vast forces of the cosmos in the first realm.

It seems that every single bird species has a resemblance to:

- an existing animal head in this third realm of the elemental world;

- a metal and planetary movement in the second realm, and;
- a cosmic force (which I cannot specify) in the first realm of the elemental world.

Some of the same can be described concerning flowers and insects.

Another interesting observation I have had relates to rain. Before, when I could observe the elemental beings of the third realm, I could observe the 'rain-beings', the entities that could be summoned, for example by the aboriginal rain dances. Now, when I enter the second realm, each rain drop appears as an individual entity, with its own elemental being and signature.

In the first realm, the enormous cosmic force creating the rain reveals itself – a force which to me, at the present time, is not individualized. This individual existence of the rain-drops shows itself physically, in sensitive crystallization, as when the snow-flakes are formed in the air. They are all different!

When I am looking at clouds and cloud formations, I can then go deeper into them. Here, I first experience or see the elementals of form, of structure. Then, in the second realm, the forces of nature, and in the first realm, 'meaning' pours forth – meaning such as the destiny of our lives or of world happenings.

Another very strange and interesting change happened to me recently in relation to *thinking, feeling* and *will, especially in relation to will*. For a long time I have been able to observe clairvoyantly the etheric streams in the body related to thinking and feeling. I have thought about will, but as Steiner said that will is a very hidden and misunderstood force, I have never actually looked to perceive this force. Then, suddenly I could see the will-forces streaming in my arms and legs. It was not a slight and diffuse vision – it was very clear and strong, and it was possible to repeat it!

*

If I concentrate my sight on an artificial phenomenon like electric light, some very different areas of the hidden worlds appear. When I thus look at an *electric bulb* shining in my living room, I first see:

1. the material and light-giving bulb. Then (going deeper),
2. the elemental being of the third realm, connected to the ahrimanic (and luciferic) forces of the light, looking like the moving and ever-changing heads of demonic entities. Then (going deeper),

3. the adversarial elemental being(s) of the second realm, which look like black, thin lines, zig-zagging the whole room. Then (going deeper),
4. a dark area of the solar system appears, as if I see behind the sun's domain, to an 'anti-sun'. Then (going deeper),
5. the same dark force appears, but now related to the whole cosmos.

When I am in a room lit with many fluorescent tubes and then go to the second realm of the elemental world, the whole room appears as a picture of modern art, with a lot of black lines traversing the canvas (or room) in all directions.

Going to the first realm, the whole space is filled up with a darkness that is overwhelming and frightening. In this darkness, many spider-like beings are living, and I have the clear impression that this is the building up of the Eighth Sphere of the Earth. Holding this Eighth Sphere in my consciousness, and directing my gaze also to the other planets of the solar system, it has become clear to me that the planets also have their ahrimanic constructions, resembling the Earth's Eighth Sphere.

It might be that some understanding of quantum physics may surface and suffice in the understanding of these phenomena. The laws of quantum physics are, in my view, related to the interface between the first and second realms of the elemental world. We know from quantum physics that human consciousness is of crucial importance. The first realm of the elemental world relates to the vast cosmic space, and thus exists only as a possibility so long as our consciousness does not penetrate this first elemental realm.

The universe is full of dark matter, which might be its elemental/ethereal potential, not (yet) grasped by the conscious mind (or the understanding of scientists).

Colours and 'breathing light'

When we enter the different areas of the spiritual world, we are no longer defined by our body. It is only here, in the material world, that we are inside our bodies, defined by our materiality and skin. In any of the spiritual realms, we merge with the area or realm in which we are – we become a part of that area. This might be frightening if we happen to enter a demonic area, but we always have to remember that *we are ourselves,* no matter what happens. In this way, we start to 'take in' the surrounding entities and powers, and we give our own powers and structure to the surroundings. Thus, we start to *breathe the structure* and powers in the realm within which we are.

- In the third realm of the elemental world, we breathe structure and colours – coloured structure.
- In the second realm of the elemental world, we breathe coloured tones – coloured vibrations.
- In the first realm of the elemental world, we breathe strong light, radiant light, although this light is hidden in darkness.

The colours in the second realm of the elemental world are sharper and brighter than those in the etheric world, where they are more like diffuse pastel colours. To me, they are more like Newton described them, whereas in the etheric world they are more like Goethe described them. This seems to be very significant – the intensity of the colours, the shapes and the environment itself.

- The adversarial aspect makes it sharp, with clear borders, strong light and colours, clear and defined tones.
- The Christ or spiritual aspect makes it go soft, undefined, somewhat blurry, with no defined borders, and more like 'cosmic' music and tones.

'Refined breathing' within the First, Second and Third Elemental Realms

Rudolf Steiner started his teaching of the aforementioned nineteen lessons of the First Class by describing the human condition in the physical. In the first lecture, on 15 February 1924, he states:

> *Where on earth's foundation, colour upon colour*
> *Life creative manifests itself;*
> *Where from earthly substance, form on form,*
> *The lifeless world takes on its finished shape;*
> *Where sentient beings, strong in will,*
> *Delight in the warming glow of their existence;*
> *Where you, O man, derive your body*
> *From earth and air and light.*

This mantra has always caught my attention, and I felt it to be especially important. Why does the (material) body originate from earth, air and light? It was not until recently that I began to understand this. Then, I saw the following with my own 'eyes':

- The third realm of the elemental world is characterized by coloured forms, as if existing in the realm of the earth.
- The second realm of the elemental world is characterized by lofty beings hurrying in horizontal movement, just like the birds flying in the air – flying in coloured sounds.
- The first realm of the elemental world is characterized by shining light, so bright and colourful that it is impossible to actually see the beings living or existing there.

As I have interpreted from Rudolf Steiner's descriptions:

- The third realm of the elemental world is the 'world of coloured forms'.
- The second realm of the elemental world is 'a world of free sounding tones'.
- The first realm of the elemental world is 'a world of shining colours'.*

*

In my book Experiences from the Threshold *I described the process of seeing into the third realm of the elemental world. Here, I will refer to some observations which relate to this world, as they throw some light on the relationship between the elements of the physical world and the elemental beings of the third realm of the elementary world.*

A description of the inhabitants of the third realm of the elemental world

In the third realm of the elemental world there are very many kinds of elemental beings, but four main groups stand out. They are the beings of:

- fire, called the salamanders;
- air, called the sylphs;

---

* Note that Steiner describes the colours in the elemental world as 'shining'. In my experience, in the pure etheric world one would characterize them as 'pastel'.

- water, called the undines;
- earth, called the gnomes.

Fire, air, earth and water are the four basic elements of nature. Within each of the four elements there are three realms or levels of elemental beings. The beings of the third realm are often called *nature spirits.*

All the elemental beings, of all three realms together, are the spiritual essence of that element. They are made up of etheric substance that is unique and specific to their particular element, but as this etheric substance is imprisoned with the adversarial beings, it looks very different from pure or genuine etheric substance. This can be seen or heard especially in the quality of their colours and their sounds. The colours are brighter and shinier, and the sounds are sharper and louder than those in the pure etheric world.

The entities of the third realm often resemble the human shape. These elemental beings work primarily on the mental plane and are known as 'builders of form'. Their speciality is to translate thought-forms into physical forms by transforming spiritual patterns firstly into astral patterns, then pseudo-etheric patterns and finally physical patterns.

They are not immortal. When their work is finished, they are absorbed back into the *ocean of Spirit.* They live a very long time – 300 to 1,000 years – and have the power to change their size and appearance at will. They cannot, however, change elements, like the elemental spirits of the second realm can.

Earth – Gnomes
The nature spirits of the earth are called gnomes. Billions of elemental beings (from the first, second and third realms) tend the earth through the cycles of the four seasons, and see to it that all living things are supplied with their daily needs.

Fire – Salamanders
The salamanders are the spirits of fire. Without these beings, fire cannot exist. You cannot light a match without a salamander being present. There are many families of salamanders, differing in size, appearance and dignity. Some people have seen them as small balls of light, but most commonly they are perceived as being lizard-like in shape and about a foot or more in length. Salamanders are considered the strongest and most powerful of all the elementals. They have

the ability to extend their size or diminish it, as required. If you ever need to light a campfire in the wilderness, call to the salamanders and they will help you.

Air – Sylphs

Sylphs are air elementals of the third realm. They live to be hundreds of years old, often reaching 1,000 without appearing to age! They are said to live on the tops of mountains. Sylphs often assume human form, but only for short periods of time. They vary in size, from being as large as a human to something much smaller. They are volatile and changeable. The winds are their particular vehicle. They work through the gases and ethers of the earth and are kind towards humans. They are usually seen with wings, looking like cherubs or fairies.

Water – Undines

Undines are the elemental beings that create the waves, the sea-streams and all the movements of the water. The substantiality of water, the composing of water itself, is more a creation of the elementals of the second realm of the elemental world. They are able to control, to a greater degree, the course and function of the water element. Etheric in nature, they exist within water itself, and this is why they can't be seen with normal physical vision. These beings are beautiful to look at and are very graceful. They are often seen riding the waves of the ocean. They can also be found in rocky pools and in marshlands. They are clothed in shimmering substances resembling water, but shining with all the colours of the sea, predominantly green. The concept of the mermaid is connected with these elemental beings. The undines also work with the plants that grow under the water and with the motion of water. Some undines inhabit waterfalls whilst others live in rivers and lakes.

Human beings and the elementals are thus trapped in our own worlds – the elemental beings in the elemental realms, as ahrimanic, luciferic and azuric entities, and the humans in the material realm, balancing between the ahrimanic and luciferic forces.

The only way to a redemption and liberation of both sides is for the human being to spiritualize, so that both sides may reunite with the help of the Christ force.

A conversation with the 'hidden people' and the elves of Iceland

This story was told to me by both the elves and the 'hidden people' of Iceland. Both accounts correspond in the main essentials.

We must remember first of all that the material existence of the human being depends upon the sacrifice of the ahrimanic, the luciferic and also the azuric beings – of all three elemental realms. Without them coming into relationship with human development, the incarnation of man in the material realm would have been impossible. All the inhabitants of the sub-human elemental realms are of an adversarial nature. The gnomes, elves, salamanders, sylphs and undines are all luciferic/ahrimanic beings. This is simultaneously beneficial and dangerous.

So, on to the creational story of the elemental inhabitants themselves, as given to me by the elder of one elf colony and two colonies of 'the hidden people' in Iceland. These words are not mine. They come directly from the elves and the hidden people themselves:

> *In the first beginning, the humans together with the whole world*
> *existed only in the spiritual realm, in the upper and lower realm of*
> *Devachan. There were no elemental realms and no etheric realm.*
> *Nothing was material and only a warm etheric fluid existed. The*
> *cosmic plan, however, was that the known world should material-*
> *ize in the material realm. In order to be able to enter or penetrate*
> *into the material realm, it was necessary to make a division in the*
> *etheric, just as God made a split in the waters on the second day*
> *of creation. One part was kept in the etheric and one part was*
> *expelled into the material realm* as the elemental/inner etheric*
> *foundation of the same. The material part was then, as a conse-*
> *quence of this split, mirror-wise, as all material is a mirroring of*
> *the spiritual, created upside-down. That is why humans always*
> *see the etheric phenomena as in a mirror. It is really the material*
> *world that is upside-down. This split is today seen in the turning*
> *of the foetus in the third week of embryology. The cosmic etheric*

---

* 1:1 In the beginning God created the heavens and the earth. 1:2 And the earth was waste and void; and darkness was upon the face of the deep: and the Spirit of God moved upon the face of the waters. 1:3 And God said, Let there be light: and there was light. 1:4 And God saw the light, that it was good: and God divided the light from the darkness. (Genesis 1.)

forces are both threefold, fourfold, sevenfold and twelvefold. The threefoldness, constituted of thinking, feeling and will, reflects especially the division of the elves, as they are likewise split into three groups, although they cooperate perfectly. This shows that in the elemental realm the entanglement of the three cosmic forces are not as in the material realm, where they are intertwined. The blue elves are masters of spiritual thinking, the yellow ones of cosmic feeling and the red ones of cosmic will.

We are thus trapped in each of our worlds. The elves in the etheric realm as ahrimanic entities and the humans in the material realm, balancing between the ahrimanic and the luciferic (and later also the azuric). The only way to a redemption and liberation of both sides is for the material human to spiritualize – to understand the elemental world, penetrate the elemental world with his thinking, feeling and will – so that both sides may reunite with the help of the Christ force.

The elfish future

The elves will be stuck in the elemental world unless humans are able to spiritualize their thinking, their will and their feeling. If this doesn't happen, then the elemental beings will be stuck in their world, the humans in their material world, and the animals will be stuck at their level of development, as the creation story of the animals is somewhat similar to that of the elves – a sort of splitting off from human development. The whole cosmos is thus dependent on the spiritualization of man. For this future to be possible, Christ helps man to create a new spiritual centre in the body. A new chakra. Not the old one, related to the spinal upwards-moving stream. Not the one in front of the heart, but one just below and behind the heart, which can be reached only by passing the heart and then turning back. This is the great mystery of 'the turning back'.

The elvish elder was very specific about this, and he even showed me, with his hands, how to reach this new spiritual centre of the heart. As described above, the human realm or world is upside-down compared to the etheric realm. Although we see the elves as standing on the ground, they really don't touch our world with the soles of their feet. Their whole existence – cities, houses and gardens – are within the earth, the rocks and the mountains. Our planet is their heaven and our cosmos is their planet or ground. This is the same as we experience when we die. Our interior becomes the whole cosmos and the whole cosmos becomes our interior.

That the cosmos is endless is thus an illusion of the material world. But the illusion of endlessness is created by the fact that both the elemental, the etheric and the physical cosmos are created or organized as a mixture of fractals and holistic constructions – as a hall of mirrors – both in themselves and between each other. This last explanation by the elfish elder confused me a little; the content threatened to exceed my understanding.

Our conversations took two to three hours in earthly time, but the above is a summary of what the elves and the hidden ones told me.

Studying a traditional Norwegian Stave church in relation to the inhabitants of the third realm of the elemental world

The first thing I observed when I went towards the old Norwegian Stave church in Bygdøy, Oslo (having 'activated' my clairvoyance) was that the church was made up of four layers, similar to a cream cake. Each layer was inhabited by different elemental beings. The first layer contained the gnomes, the second the undines, the third the sylphs and the final (and top) layer contained the salamanders.

- The gnome elemental beings in the first and bottom layer (although being entities of the third elemental realm, also, as its life force, expressing the life ether of the inner etheric world) moved slowly in a circle 'with' the sun.
- The undine-elemental beings in the second layer (although being entities of the third elemental realm, also, as its life force, expressing the chemical ether of the inner etheric world) moved slowly in a circle 'against' the sun.
- The sylph-elemental beings in the third layer (although being entities of the third elemental realm, also, as its life force, expressing the light ether of the inner etheric world) moved slowly in a circle again 'with' the sun.
- The salamander-elemental beings in the fourth and upper layer (although being entities of the third elemental realm, also, as its life force, expressing the warmth ether of the inner etheric world) moved slowly in a circle again 'against' the sun.

These elemental beings are related to a fourfold division of the third realm of the elemental world, but as all living entities, they use etheric energy or force derived from the inner etheric world, a world that is not far away from this third realm of the elemental world, and to where these beings long to be. Perhaps they long even more to be in the outer etheric world, where the 'real' spiritual beings can be found, and where the Christ-force can be experienced.

Norwegian Stave church at Bygdøy, Oslo

When we entered the church, we could, to my great astonishment, see physical signs of the four kinds of elemental beings painted on the walls, exactly at the same levels as the elemental beings were operating:

- *Quadrats* (four-sides) are expressions of the gnomes, or the life-element of the etheric world present in the elemental world.
- *Half-moons* are expressions of the undines, or the chemical-element (also called 'tone' element) of the etheric world, present in the elemental world.
- *Triangles* are expressions of the sylphs, or the light-element of the etheric world, present in the elemental world.
- *Circles* or spheres are expressions of the salamanders, or the warmth element of the etheric world, present in the elemental world.

Experiences at a music festival

I will now give you a short description of my spiritual experiences at a Classical Music Festival held in Sandefjord (Norway). Twenty-three top musicians played music from Shostakovich, Pärt, Tüür (who was the festival composer and was present himself), Beethoven, Satie, Prokofiev, Debussy, Stravinsky, Antheil, Schubert, Mozart, Brahms and Dukas. What I observed clearly was that several of the pieces of music were made up of three or four parts, and that each part often represented or created one of the ethers – either the water, light, earth or life ether – brought down into the elemental world by the music. The musicians were not magicians with the power to bring the etheric forces and forms all the way into the material world – that is maybe for future musicians!

I started to observe that each piece of music created or built an elemental structure of the third realm of the elemental world, within the room where the musicians were playing. This creation resembled the structure of the Stave church in many ways, as it mostly contained all the four elements in a certain harmonious inner structure and relationship. I also observed that the music from the 'great' composers created a harmonious building, constructed from all the four elements mirroring the etheric ethers, whereas the music from the 'lesser' composers was lacking parts or bits of the harmonious elemental structure.

In the beginning of each piece of music – in the first part – a structure was created that resembled a foundation – just as when a foundation is laid when building a house. In the second and third parts, this structure started to be filled with flowing forms, often with a certain colour (chemical or light ether – water-element or air-element). In the fourth part of the music (if it was constructed with four parts), it was crowned with the warmth ether, the fire element of the salamanders.

For some of the composers, one of the elements/ethers was totally missing, so that the building or construction stood unfinished or unfulfilled. I will not criticize any of the composers, but will comment that the buildings of Beethoven, Mozart, Tüür and Stravinsky were the best to look at.

- Beethoven's music built up Tibetan cultural forms: temples with dragon-forms and Himalayan mountains.
- Mozart's built Gothic cathedrals with angelic forms.
- Stravinsky's music built low buildings that in the end were crushed and destroyed. Could this relate to the time he lived with the destructiveness of Stalin?
- Tüür built quite small, cabin-like constructions with no communication between them.

And then, at the end, the unavoidable and undesirable clapping, the applause, destroyed and took down all the beautiful constructions! I hate clapping, and discourage it at all of my events.

Observations regarding the production of biodynamic preparations

Rudolf Steiner gave his agricultural course in Koberwitz (now Kobierzye, Poland), from 7 to 16 June 1924.* There, he described how one can and ought to help the earth and the world to be aware of the cosmic influences. One of the most important tools in this work are the biodynamic preparations, of which there are seven, made as follows:

1. Oak-bark inside the cranium of a cow.
2. Nettles buried in the earth.
3. Yarrow inside the bladder of a deer.

---

* *Agriculture Course*, op. cit.

4. Manure in the horn of a cow.
5. Plant-juice of Valerian Officinalis.
6. Dandelion in the mesentery of a cow.
7. Chamomile inside a cow's intestines.

All preparations made, re-modelled or strengthened certain parts, organs or abilities of the gnome elementals in such a way that they could be more beneficial to agriculture. I have observed the following:

- The nettle-preparation produces elemental beings with especially big eyes.
- Yarrow inside the bladder of a deer enlarges the 'kidneys' of the elementals, so that they become sensitive to the astral forces.
- Chamomile inside the cow intestines gives a 'body-tasting' ability.
- Oak-bark inside the cranium of a cow activates the vomeronasal organ* – an organ that science doesn't yet know the effect of.
- Manure in the horn of a cow activates the whole digestive apparatus.
- Dandelion in the mesentery (omentum majus) of a cow activates the observation of the cosmic forces, especially the stars.
- The plant-juice of Valerian Officinalis elevates the sensibility of the skin.

In this way, the heap of compost could be transformed into a sensing organism, serving the dying earth, but as we have seen, the presence of Christ is necessary, and biodynamic agriculture has not yet fully come to realize this.

Seeing into the second realm of the elemental world

In the works of Rudolf Steiner, it is sometimes difficult to distinguish which realm of the elemental world he is describing. But now,

---

* The vomeronasal organ (VNO), or Jacobson's organ, is the paired auxiliary olfactory (smell) sense organ located in the soft tissue of the nasal septum, in the nasal cavity just above the roof of the mouth (the hard palate). It is present and functional in all snakes and lizards, and in many mammals, including cats, dogs, cattle, pigs and some primates; in humans it is present, but is vestigial and non-functional.

as I have experienced these three realms to a certain degree, I think I have a tentative view on this. In each of the three realms, there appear to be:

- a different kind of initiation;
- a different kind of clairvoyance;
- different forces;
- different possibilities of exerting magic (occultism);
- different realms of the cosmos;
- different parts of our soul;
- different movements;
- different parts of our body; and
- different soul abilities.

In the second realm, the relationships are definitely towards atomic structures of materiality, to the planetary system, to a right-left movement and to inspirative faculties. Further, the relationships are to the second hierarchy of angelic beings (through the Archangels) and to the metals – as these are some of the few material substances that exist in an atomic state and not in a molecular state. As the third elemental realm is related to the structure of material beings, the second elemental realm is related to a deeper structure, a deeper 'meaning' of creation.

Now, after having discovered the three elemental realms, when I look up at the clouds in the sky, at water or the flight of birds, I often observe a pattern of meaning that I have never seen or observed before. This structure or pattern relates to the atomic structure of material creation. This structure of creation also expresses itself in coloured tones. In observing these consciously, it feels like the coloured tones become incorporated in a sort of breathing through the ears, as if my ears and also the rest of my soul become entangled in this weaving in coloured tones.

At this point I will add a peculiar observation that I made after being able to observe the second realm, that has to do with the leaves of trees. In the autumn, very many leaves of different trees become brightly coloured, and even many plants show this change when the days and nights become colder. When I was in school, we learnt that this change in colouration was not really a 'willed' change. We were told that the trees and plants had to take care of and conserve the chlorophyll molecules for the following year, and that they actively transported these molecules down into their roots for use the following spring – in a way similar to how humans take care of the iron in the hemoglobin molecule. Thus, when the green chlorophyll disappears from the leaves, the red and yellow coloured substances, that had been there all the time, could now be seen, as the green no longer 'covered' them up.

For a long time, this explanation made sense to me. Then I read in a scientific journal that this was not true. The coloured substances of autumn were *actively produced* by the tree or plant itself. Also, it was reported that this production of coloured substances used quite a lot of energy, so it had to be sufficiently important for the trees and plants to carry out this process. Science had no idea why this was done, and neither had I, but I wondered about it for many years.

Then, after being able to observe the second realm of the elemental world, one day I understood why. I stood observing how the earth breathes in during the autumn, how the etheric forces are breathed into the earth and stay there during the winter, as described by Rudolf Steiner in his *Agriculture Course*. But then I observed another aspect of this etheric 'substance', or rather force – a more spiritual-ized version of it, a sort of astralized part of the etheric body of the plant. This astralized version, this lighter part, did not sink down into the earth. Rather, it lifted upwards; it started to ascend into the spiritual world, the astral part of the spiritual world. But it could not do this without a coloured springboard – without the help of bright colours. Without these colours, this lighter part of the etheric plant- or tree-body would be lost to the astral spirituality. The trees con-tribute in this way to the upbuilding of the celestial heaven, to the new Jerusalem, so to say, and that is why they use so much energy to build the coloured substances.

Rudolf Steiner described much the same in relation to butterflies – how all the time they let spiritual substances 'evaporate' up into the spiritual world. Even birds do something of the same when they die. Maybe that is why butterflies have to create colours?

With this in mind, we find hugely interesting indications by Rudolf Steiner, about how etheric forces and elemental beings are released or changed by breaking down and building up nutritional molecules in digestion (breaking down molecules) and in metabo-lism (both building up and breaking down of molecules), and also how we can be initiated through *metals by their atomic structure* (my interpretation).

Further Reflections on the Elemental Realms

- The third elemental kingdom had to live in the duality of light and darkness, in which Christ could later create a balance, through the soul of the human being.
- The second elemental kingdom had to live in the duality of warmth and cold, in which Christ could later create a balance, through the soul of the human being.
- The first elemental kingdom had to live in the duality of life and death, in which Christ could later create a balance, through the soul of the human being.

Electricity, magnetism, atomic energy and vacuum-energy were also created at the same time as the three elemental realms:

- During Hyperborea, the light entered further into the darkness and became electricity.
- During Lemuria, coldness entered further into warmth, and became magnetism.
- With the Atlantean epoch, the life ether entered the solid Earth element and the death forces, and became atomic energy.
- During the post-Atlantean period, the ethers entered all the way through each of the three elemental realms and into the outer etheric world, and became vacuum energy.

We thus have the super-physical and the sub-physical ethers. Three levels of materiality were then created as follows:

- *The constructions of materiality:* are created through the third hierarchy of angelic beings. This level is made up of all entities, all machines like cars, 5G-towers, and so on. Here work the elemental beings of light and darkness, and lay the foundation of hygienic occultism.
- *The atomic layer:* is created through the second hierarchy of angelic beings. Here we have the molecules, the combination of atoms, making up myriad 'things' in the material universe. Here work the elemental beings of cold and warmth, and lay the foundation of mechanical occultism.
- *The layer of vacuum:* is created through the first hierarchy of angelic beings, the first hierarchy of angelic activity – of course, 'overshone' by the Christ force or being. It might help to include in this layer the vacuum described by quantum

physics. Here work the elemental beings of death and life, which lay the foundation of eugenic occultism.

There is only and always harmony in the second and the first realms of the elemental kingdom. The spirits of hindrance only come into play with the Dynamis and only with the start of Old Moon. In the molecular layer, one sees the activity of the chemical/tone/number ether, and behind this one can see the activity of the second hierarchy. The working upon the material, the spiritualizing of matter, belongs to human beings working with the first hierarchy.

These realms and layers relate to the three celestial realms above us:

- *The third angelic realm:* this consists of the creators of the third elemental realm of nature: the Angels, the Archangels and the Archai.
- *The second angelic realm:* consists of the creator of forms and movement and wisdom of the creation: the Exusiai, Dynamis and Kyriotetes. They are the creators of the second elemental realm.
- *The first angelic realm:* are the mighty creators of all matter, of the atomic world, and consist of the Thrones, the Cherubim and the Seraphim. They are the creators of the first realm of the elemental world.

The first hierarchy works within the interior of the earth. Similarly, in the human being, the ego works (today) upon the physical body, upon the salts and sugars eaten, upon the mineral kingdom.

We can then understand the three realms or layers of occultism:

- *Hygienic occultism:* which deals with regulating the powers present in living beings, the beings of the third realm of creation, as animals and man. The powers to be regulated are the luciferic and the ahrimanic forces* and the elemental beings of light and darkness. The only regulator is the Christ force. This occultism belongs mainly to the third realm of the elemental world.

---

* The Christ forces work as balance to the luciferic and the ahrimanic forces. And the Christ forces work in direct opposition to the azuric forces. Yes, hygienic occultism will need to restore the balance and find ways to oppose the azuric forces!

- *Mechanical occultism:* is about bringing the atomic force in resonance with the forces of both the first and third elemental realm of existence, which again can be put in action by the 'I'-force of human beings, as long as this 'I' can receive its force from the Christ. This occultism belongs mainly to the second realm of the elemental world, where also quantum-mechanics may be placed, as well as the effects of homeopathy. The powers here are the next highest realm of the luciferic and the ahrimanic forces and the elemental beings of warmth and coldness. The only regulator is still the Christ force.
- *Eugenic occultism:* deals with the construction and ensoulment of the foetus and the incarnation of the spirit. The powers to be regulated are the highest realm of the azuric forces in cooperation with the luciferic and the ahrimanic forces, and the elemental beings of life and death. The only regulator is still the Christ force.

Chapter 3

How the Adversarial Forces Hinder
Spiritual Observation
Corrupting our Spiritual Senses

I would suggest that most people believe that the explosion of technological advances has seen the heralding of a new era of profound evolution. With the push of a few buttons, anything and everything can be found, researched, bought and sold. In addition, our ability to connect immediately with one another through social media has morphed the concept of the written word. Language has now taken on a divisiveness of monumental proportions, as instant digital communication and online 'trolling' has become the most effective weapon since the invention of the gun. So, it is no wonder that the existence of electronic technology has also created an effective tool for the blossoming of adversarial forces. I will try to explain the exact methodology through which Ahriman, as the primary sinister force, can manipulate the devices of this technology to gain control over the future of humanity. His major access point is through the portals created by our sense organs.

Rudolf Steiner has described thoroughly the existence of twelve human senses.* He described that each of these faculties act as openings or portals to the physical, etheric and astral aspects of both man and the cosmos in which we live. Each sense is connected to one of the divine beings of the first hierarchy, expressed in each of the twelve signs of the zodiac. In this way, they can be viewed as a twelvefold entity.

In Steiner's description of human beings, he categorizes our make up using several methods. First, he divides us into four layers, consisting of our physical, etheric, astral and 'I' sheaths. However, this concept of a fourfold being can further be described as having both seven and even nine levels, if one also considers our spiritual future as including the higher levels referred to (in Eastern terminology) as Buddhi, Manas and Atma. Ultimately, our higher selves, as well as all of creation, are governed by a primary trinity of the powerful soul

---

* See lecture of 20 June 1916, Berlin, in *Towards Imagination*, SteinerBooks 1990.

faculties of thinking, feeling and will. They represent the fundamental processes in which our cosmos is organized and developed, and weave themselves into all aspects of Creation. This trinity encompasses the entire cosmos, the divine angelic hierarchies, as well as the 'under-nature' world of spiritual beings such as elves, hidden people and other elementals relating to the third level of the elemental world. In addition, we have the beings of the second realm, and the forces of the first.

The third aspect (realm) of our elemental universe:
This can be seen with the spiritual eye as an upside-down version of the physical world (or perhaps it could be our world that is upside down!). In this way, one could imagine that our feet were to contact their reverse image beneath the spiritual earth. Thus, the orientation is up-down.

The second aspect (realm) of our elemental universe:
This can be seen with the spiritual eye as a reality that is 90^0 to the third realm, that is 90^0 to our material body. The orientation is right-left.

The first aspect (realm) of our elemental universe:
This can be seen with the spiritual eye as a different reality, living in a fluid and always changing medium. The orientation is front-back.

The three cosmic forces of thinking, feeling and will play a role in every aspect of our lives. They are revealed within the anthroposophical medical system as the three fundamental poles of the nerve-sensory system (thinking), the rhythmic system (feeling) and the metabolic/muscular/skeletal system (will).* However, it is of paramount importance that we understand that this template can also be applied to the twelve senses, particularly when we consider the steps toward spiritual initiation known as *Imagination* (the four physical senses of touch, life, movement and orientation), *Inspiration* (the four soul senses of smell, taste, temperature and sight), and *Intuition* (the four spiritual senses of hearing, speech, thought and perception of the 'I' of others).

---

* See Rudolf Steiner and Ita Wegman, *Extending Practical Medicine*, Rudolf Steiner Press 2000.

The senses described by Steiner are extremely complex formations, as they exhibit both an outward and an inward direction of
flow. For example, the eyes that perceive the cosmos send an outward etheric stream, enabling them also to receive an inward flow of
information from the thing they are viewing. It is a general spiritual
rule that any movement automatically creates a countermovement,
and this is even relevant for time.

The twelve senses are also developed in the luciferic, ahrimanic,
azuric and human karmic doppelgängers. These four entities employ
the senses in a unique way. The human karmic doppelgänger uses
the physical sense organs as we use them in the material world.
The ahrimanic, azuric and luciferic doppelgängers, however, create their own mirror images of these structures. The template that
ahrimanic and azuric forces utilize are situated deeper within the
physical body, whilst the luciferic templates are more superficial,
infiltrating the astral sheath. For example, in the eye, the ahrimanic
sense organ lies about one cm behind the material optic structure,
while the luciferic is in front of the eye. I perceive the ahrimanic
structure with my clairvoyant ability as a greyish structure, similar
to a tin plate.

These structures are also activated and developed by viewing
electronic screens. From this information, it can be surmised that
there are actually three aspects of each of these sense organs. If one
considers all twelve sense organs and combines the fact that each of
these senses are employed by three doppelgängers (including ourselves), and that each organ is involved in both an outgoing and
an ingoing stream, we conclude that we are actually dealing with
72 qualities in total that should be considered when understanding
sensory functions! Note that all twelve senses can observe spiritu-
ally. If the spiritual eye is developed, for example, we refer to its
ability as clairvoyance.

The eye:
The first sense I will discuss here is the eye, the foundation of sight
and also very central to Imagination and clairvoyance. Regarding the
eye as a physical organ, I have observed that when viewing a living
object, especially in nature, the inhabitants of higher spiritual hierarchies also share the observation. I have also found that the sense
organs with little or no fat, such as the eye, have a stronger affinity
for the etheric. However, when one is observing the screen of a cell

phone, the observations are intertwined with another reality, where colours diminish and ahrimanic forces dominate.

Regarding the effect of the presence of Lucifer and Ahriman on our sense organ of sight – whether we are observing the results of these demonic influences on the nature of the physical world, or on the under-nature (under-world, elemental world) of the virtual electronic world – I find that both adversarial forces can thrive on the latter, including the internet, artificial light, LED displays, computer monitors and cell phones. This is described in the (two volume) series by Paul Emberson entitled *From Gondishapur to Silicon Valley*. While the adversaries such as Lucifer and Ahriman are able to take part in this under-world via electronics, handwriting is a safer alternative for communication, as it is under the domain of the Angels.

The strength of these doppelgängers is woven into one's sensory observations. Paul Emberson claims that the use of computers stimulates the adversarial forces' strong hold on our existence. For example, if one views a movie, this action will actually strengthen the ahrimanic doppelgänger's visual sense organ. As mentioned above, this eye is grey and large, similar in appearance to a plate made of tin. In 1917, Steiner addressed his concern about attending a movie theatre.* He describes that the eyes of those watching a film take on the sense organs of Ahriman.

The touch/feeling of the skin:
The second sense I would like to discuss is that of touch/feeling. The related organ to this sense at the physical level is the skin. My observations regarding this organ date back to well before my understanding of anthroposophy. During the first years of my veterinary studies at Oslo University, I spent some time between classes observing the tourists, especially those that were overweight. With my spiritual

---

* 'So when people are sitting in the cinema, what they see there comes to reside within them not through their ordinary faculties of perception but at a deeper material level than is normal for the process of perception. A person becomes etherically goggle-eyed. His eyes begin to look like those of a seal, only much bigger, when he watches lots of films. I mean etherically bigger. This has an effect not only on what lives in his conscious mind but it has a materializing influence on his sub-consciousness.' Lecture of 27 February 1917, from *Building Stones for an Understanding of the Mystery of Golgotha*, Rudolf Steiner Press 2015.

eye, I saw that in many of those people their skin (the outside of their body) was in front of a withdrawn etheric sheath. The fatty tissue was in a way hanging loose, outside of the etheric field. Thus, the effect of the sense organ that allows *clairsentience* was diminished. In other words, being overweight or fat has an effect on supra-sensory feeling (to be able to *feel* spiritual realities). Therefore, when a person goes on a weight reduction programme, it may be possible to develop the spiritual sense of touch, as the etheric sheath expands in an outward direction, thus diminishing the stranglehold of Ahriman and Lucifer on this particular sense organ.

With the physical sense organ of the skin, as well as its luciferic and ahrimanic templates, we should understand how Rudolf Steiner described clairvoyance as a relationship between the physical body, the etheric body and the astral body, especially when the spiritual bodies are 'outside' the physical form. For example, during the time of Atlantis, the etheric sheath of the head was outside its physical counterpart. In this way, Atlanteans were clairvoyant and able to observe the etheric world. However, if the etheric body is 'within' the physical body, the supersensible sense organs become muted.

It should also be noted that the azuric adversaries tend to linger in the area of the stomach, just where many people tend to gain weight.

*

It appears that the ahrimanic and luciferic sense organs are developing in synch with our growing love of technology, especially over the past twenty years. As Goethe wrote that the sun created the need for human eyes, so will the existence of virtual media and electronic devices create the need for an ahrimanic eye. I have observed that children are developing a special affinity for understanding and connecting to such devices, as their doppelgänger-eye becomes more sophisticated. The healthy spiritual forces, in contrast, avoid such devices, creating a dissolution in healthy social connections amongst the population.

An even more sinister connotation lies in our inability to advance our goal toward spiritual initiation through the processes of Imagination, Inspiration and Intuition. Therefore, we should proceed with caution and limit electronic communications in our daily life, including the use of email and social media. Our soul life, etheric life and physical bodies depend on it. We need to protect our future now, for our children but also for the future of the spirit of humanity as a whole.

Corrupting our general clairvoyance:
The ahrimanic, azuric and luciferic beings, including their masters Ahriman, Lucifer and Sorat fear the growing etheric clairvoyance of human beings – especially clairvoyance in the *second and first* realm of the elemental world. Lucifer and Ahriman fear that human beings will be able to develop clairvoyance, because then they will be able eventually to traverse the elemental world and find the Christ in the outer etheric realm, as it is here that Christ will show himself as promised (see Acts, Chapter 1, verses 6-11).[*] This is called the Second Coming, and it will happen in the clouds, that is, in the outer etheric realm. Rudolf Steiner stated this as follows:

> The being whom we call Christ once walked the earth in flesh and blood at the beginning of our era. He will never again return in a physical body, for that was a unique event and will not be repeated. But He will come again in an etheric form in the period I have mentioned. People will learn to perceive Christ by virtue of growing towards him through this etheric perception.[†]

Two of the most important concepts in anthroposophical literature are:

- Christ's Second Coming in the etheric; and
- humanity's collective passage over the threshold of the spiritual world.

---

[*] Now having met together, they asked him, 'Lord, has the time come for you to restore the kingdom to Israel?' He replied, 'It is not for you to know times or dates that the Father has decided by his own authority, but you will receive the power of the Holy Spirit which will come on you, and then you will be my witnesses not only in Jerusalem but throughout Judaea and Samaria, and indeed to earth's remotest end.' As he said this he was lifted up while they looked on, and a cloud took him from their sight. They were still staring into the sky as he went, when suddenly two men in white were standing beside them, and they said, 'Why are you Galileans standing here looking into the sky? This Jesus who has been taken up from you into heaven will come back in the same way as you have seen him go to heaven.'

[†] See *The Second Coming of Christ*, Rudolf Steiner Press 2008.

In order for us to be able to observe this, it is of great importance that we allow the spiritual part of our sensory organs to become conscious – to be opened. Several have related this phenomenon to the activation of the chakras, especially to the heart chakra. In this context I will focus on the changes we can expect to observe in our twelve sensory organs.

The reason why this is so important is that, as Christ reveals himself in the etheric, we need to have organs to observe this, or else this event will pass by unnoticed, which will have catastrophic consequences for mankind. Therefore, the opposing powers will do their utmost to prevent us from being able to observe this incident.

Early in the year 1910, Rudolf Steiner spoke for the first time about the mystery of the true nature of Christ's Second Coming. During that year, he gave a series of lectures on this topic, and several others in the following years. The importance of this topic cannot be exaggerated. The study of the Second Coming of Christ, the collective passing of the threshold of mankind and the opening of our spiritual sensory organs are fundamental to our entire understanding. Christ's first coming in the flesh occurred in an era where human sensory organs could only observe the material reality, at the deepest point of the descent during Kali Yuga, the Dark Age. But today, our open spiritual organs will more and more be able to find Christ in the etheric. First, he will be seen only by a few, but over the next 3,000 years, more and more will be able to see him.

In a lecture in Basel on 1 October 1911,* Steiner indicated that in the future Christ would be felt or heard by all that gathered to receive him. So, the adversarial forces will try their best, in various ways, to hinder our clairvoyance so that we will not be able to find the Christ.

Some of these ways are as follows:

- To foster strong materialistic beliefs. This is discussed in many anthroposophical books and articles.
- To corrupt the senses through the developing ahrimanic, azuric or luciferic sense-organs, which open observation of the ahrimanic, azuric or luciferic worlds, instead of the real or 'good' spiritual worlds. This is discussed further in my book *Spiritual Translocation*.

---

* See 'The Etherization of the Blood' from *Esoteric Christianity and the Mission of Christian Rosenkreutz*, Rudolf Steiner Press 2000.

- To corrupt human beings' budding clairvoyance through interfering with initiation itself, by leading us to the luciferic or ahrimanic worlds instead of the 'real' spiritual world. I will now discuss this method of the adversarial forces.

The first time I was able to observe this clever strategy was at a meeting with a group of twenty-five clairvoyant persons, who met a few times a year to discuss their experiences. They were all publicly-declared clairvoyants, and all of them were active in the field, giving courses, writing books, offering personal guidance, and so on.

When I studied each person in this group, it was apparent that around 80% had an adversarial 'parasite' or 'demon' attached to them. This parasite was mostly located 90^0 to the vertical direction of the human being, as shown in the picture below – thus, an azuric entity.

Illustrating an azuric parasite inhabiting a human that believes he/she is clairvoyant (with thanks to Lizz Daniels for her artwork)

In some, this parasite was extremely strong, whilst in others it was weak. This suggests that some 80% of so-called clairvoyants – people who believe they are clairvoyant – have but a spiritual 'opening' or 'portal', created by themselves, that is used by an ahrimanic, luciferic or azuric entity. In this way, the adversarial forces are able to offer us a clairvoyance that we think is 'clean', but is actually a deceit – an erroneous way into the spiritual worlds.

We can differentiate between what kind of adversarial entity inhabits a 'corrupted' clairvoyant by the direction of the adversarial 'body'.

- The luciferic adversary has its length axis parallel to our own axis.
- The ahrimanic adversary has its length axis 90^0 to our own axis, in a right-left axis.
- The azuric adversary has its length axis 90^0 to our own axis, in a front-back axis, close to the Christ mid-point but a little further down.

The pathological dependence on technology can be changed by letting in the Christ force between the luciferic and ahrimanic forces (see the picture of Steiner's wooden sculpture – where Christ himself separates Lucifer from Ahriman, creating a balancing space – on p. 16). These forces should stay in their rightful domain. In these times, in both physical and elemental worlds, Christ cannot do this on his own – we need to help.

Postscript

Vidar's Further Teachings

In the period between the beginning of the editorial process of this book and its publication, I received the following further teachings from Vidar. At a very late stage of the schedule, the publisher kindly agreed to add these further teachings here in the form of this Postscript:

*

The very next day, the teachings continued, with Vidar describing the deeper relationships between the elemental realms and the cultural ages.

One of the intentions of the whole post-Atlantean age is that we should understand physical *Materia* or matter – just as it was for the Atlantean age to understand the etheric. To understand it, we have consciously to comprehend the three elemental realms, which are the foundation of material creation. And to understand creation consciously, we have first to lose it all, and then, in consciousness, to regain it.

At the beginning, in the first period – the Indian – the three elemental realms were open to humanity, but then a gradual darkening of the elemental realms set in, and with this also a severance from the outer etheric world. Humanity sank more and more into darkness. Human beings felt a certain loss of the spiritual connection, the outer etheric world.

As the second realm was closed, humanity increasingly became severed from the outer etheric realm. This happened in the third period of the post-Atlantean age.

Then, in the fourth period of the post-Atlantean age, the third elemental realm was closed, and we became totally shut off. Then the Turning Point of Time* appeared and a seed of salvation was given us at the year 33, as Christ entered earthly development and

---

* Rudolf Steiner uses this phrase to refer to Christ's incarnation, death and resurrection.

made it possible to reopen the three elemental realms. They would first be reopened within our consciousness in the years 1887, 1949 and 2019.

In the next period – the Russian or Slavic period – they will be reopened within our astral consciousness, as a sort of repetition of the openings we now experience, and in the following great period – the American – they will be reopened within the etheric. Finally, they will be reopened in the physical, and our whole age will end. This was Vidar's teaching that day.

He also mentioned the change in music, as music is one of the foundations of the elemental realms – together with mathematics – and is somewhat different in each realm; but this teaching was and is still somewhat unclear to me. It had to do with the harmonies of many tones, to twelve and then to seven, and then back again to innumerable tones, as in cosmic music. In the inner etheric, these numerical relationships also played a part, but in the outer etheric realm they played a minor part, or maybe none.

A personal comment – although all of this is already personal – is that during the three nights of this 'fourth period' (for me, between Sunday and Wednesday), I hardly slept at all, as a theme from Bach's *Christmas Oratorio* kept playing in my head: '... *and the darkness is shattered at Christmas time* ...'. (I guess that was during the birth of the Saviour.)

As the fourth period came to its end, it did not actually end... Vidar's Greek, godlike appearance* did not vanish or transform on Thursday, and neither on Friday. However, it did somewhat fade, and another very strange looking character appeared. It appeared from behind the Greek god, slowly walking in front of him and standing there – but the Greek god did not vanish. So, at the end of Friday and Saturday both figures appeared together.

This new figure – that according to Steiner's teachings about the succession of cultures should represent the fifth post-Atlantean period, our own period (starting in 1413 and ending

* See pp. 63-64.

in 3573) – was very different from the Greek.* It was more like a scarecrow! Something like a combination of a scarecrow, a clown and a skinny hobo.

In showing the first four figures, Vidar represented them by 'becoming' them. But this time he definitely did not become this – totally unexpected – figure. Rather, he pointed at it, indicating that it was separate. Then he stated that he did not identify at all with this creature, which he had done with the first four entities or expressions. This scarecrow appeared quite silly and a little scary. And even more so, if indeed it represents our modern culture (although with a backup from the Greek culture)!

Over the following days, I contemplated this figure and received the teachings that emanated via this creature from Vidar. The first thought I had was that it looked both dead and alive, just like a 'real' scarecrow. The words from the Apocalypse of St John that the angel speaks about Sardes[†] came to my mind. (Sardes should represent the same age or period as this scarecrow.) The angel characterized the period we're living in now as being alive… but actually dead.[‡]

---

* 'All teaching, all pedagogy, all human education, and the whole outer human life must be imbued with spiritual insights in the course of the fifth post-Atlantean epoch (1413-3573). It must be realized that what is today considered science in materialistic circles must gradually disappear with its consequences from the life of the earth. And all the struggles that will still have to be endured in the fifth post-Atlantic period will only be an outward expression of a spiritual battle, just as the present [First World] war is ultimately also an outward expression of the opposition between materialism and the spiritual world view. For however deeply things may be hidden – behind the infinitely sad events of the present time – lies the struggle of materialism against the spiritual worldview. This battle must be fought. It will take different forms, but it will have to be fought because people will have to learn to endure whatever is necessary to acquire the spiritual worldview for the sixth post-Atlantic period.' (Rudolf Steiner, lecture of 15 January 1917 in *The Karma of Untruthfulness*, Vol. 2 (Rudolf Steiner Press 2005.)

[†] The seven churches are thought to represent the seven cultural ages or periods; 1. Ephesus, 2. Smyrna, 3. Pergamum, 4. Thyatira, 5. Sardis, 6. Philadelphia, and 7. Laodicea.

[‡] 'To the angel of the church in Sardis write: These are the words of him who holds the seven spirits of God and the seven stars. I know your deeds; you have a reputation of being alive, but you are dead.' (Revelation 3)

This scarecrow figure started to frighten me. It was both dead and alive. It was both cunning and utterly stupid. It was attractive and utterly disgusting. Its hair was standing up on all sides and in all directions (just like Boris Johnson's!) and its body was skinny, without muscles and strength. The colours of its clothes were manifold and totally without harmony. Its clothes were hanging loose, without any style, with big patches all over, just like a circus clown's.

All the time this entity grew stronger whilst the Greek god grew weaker. I was now experiencing the same period that I was living in within the physical world. But it was strange. It was almost like my vision was changed – as if my surroundings had become sharper and more multi-dimensional.

Then we reached our present time… and that became a shock for me, because then I realized that the whole history of civilization and humanity was also shown through my own personal development. The whole of evolution was a synthesis of my own – and humanity's – development.

I remember that this insight also came to me when I studied the history of philosophy at the University of Oslo; I recognized my whole spiritual development and life in the life and development of Western philosophy – from my early childhood to the present day. The development of humanity and I were intertwined – they were one and the same.

These events brought on a certain depression within me. Then we reached the future. The scarecrow was now changing constantly. It became darker, bent forward and more and more animalistic – increasingly aggressive and 'evil'. Its nails and its fingers grew longer.

The next days were not pleasant. The scarecrow developed into a horrible creature; scary, ugly and dark. But in the distant surroundings a certain light began to shimmer in the thickening darkness: a faint blush of hope. Then it all started to become quite complicated.

Until now, the different representations of the various cultures had shown themselves in a change of Vidar's own appearance. Now, as this appearance became somewhat ugly, it seemed that Vidar would not – or could not – change his self into something that ugly. He was separated from the scarecrow, which appeared in front of Vidar. And simultaneously, behind Vidar, appeared an Egyptian figure, which created a kind of balancing of the scarecrow figure, who all the time grew uglier. After a couple of days, this Egyptian figure took on a certain Mesopotamian trait.

So now there were three (or four) figures on the threshold of the outer etheric world, intended to teach me about the near future. In the front was the scarecrow, growing uglier all the time; in the middle was Vidar, in companionship with Balder; and at the back was this Egyptian-Mesopotamian entity. All were seen from the 'front' of the threshold – from where one enters the spiritual realms – that is, from the elemental side. Then Vidar looked at me, saying: 'You should read the books of Seth.'

The next day, a definite change occurred with the scarecrow entity. It became more distinct, more sharply outlined, and also darker in its shadowy appearance. Simultaneously, it became more animalistic. Its fingers grew longer and sharper – like something between an amphibian and a scorpion. Then the scarecrow started to move from the place where it had stood (just in front of Vidar, on the spiritual side of the threshold – remember that this is the threshold between the first elemental realm and the outer etheric or spiritual world, or, as the elemental world is actually the physical world, the threshold between 'our' world and the spiritual world) and slowly entered the elemental world. It felt as if the scarecrow was leaving the spiritual world and had started to enter the physical world. That gave me an unpleasant feeling. I should also add that since Vidar had started to teach me about the future, I had felt a certain emptiness, a certain depression. To enter the future is a painful experience for me.

Many years ago I had developed a method to actually enter both the past and the future, as I have described in my book *Pappel*. I often entered the past, but not the future. The method was first to enter the strong etheric streams that flow between trees – an etheric realm which I consider today to be the 'inner' etheric realm. At that time, I observed them and then stepped right into them. Then I had two possibilities: to go left or right. If I moved left, I entered the past. I could travel quite far into the past, and in imaginary pictures I could observe the changing plant-forms or tree-forms. I travelled all the way to Silurian times. If I walked to the right, I entered the future. I never dared to do this. I felt the past as being filled with substance, whereas the future felt empty of this elemental substance.

And now, as Vidar – through the scarecrow creature – urged me to enter the future, I was scared. The name 'scarecrow' was quite appropriate. Also, the 'atmosphere' of the future was quite 'thin', void of air – giving me a certain difficulty with my breathing. This all gave me a feeling of displeasure. But the guardian urged me to watch and to follow.

In the first period of the future, the scarecrow transformed more and more into a fierce and dangerous wolf, almost like a werewolf. But then, the fierce wolf became more and more like a dog; and on the final day of the fifth cultural epoch, the creature seemed like an exhausted dog – not dangerous at all. This took place on Thursday evening.

Then, on the Friday morning, when the sixth post-Atlantean epoch was supposed to start, the transformed scarecrow – or rather dog – was completely gone, and the powerful face of Peter Deunov appeared... very clear and utterly distinct. The start of the sixth epoch was very different from the bloodthirsty fifth epoch.

One other difference was also that the first, second, third and fourth epochs were dominated by godlike entities. Then, the fifth epoch was dominated by a man-like entity that changed into a murdering and bloodthirsty scarecrow or werewolf-like creature; and the sixth was represented by a human being full of wisdom, compassion and spirituality. What a relief!

At this moment, I asked Vidar about the situation regarding Christ and Sophia. He then showed me an imagination that pictured the relationship between these good spiritual forces. This imagination showed me the whole etheric world encompassed in a huge shining rainbow, which was the Christ force. The ground under this rainbow was Sophia, and Vidar and Balder formed the gateway to it. Going to bed that first night was peaceful and satisfying.

The following day, the image of Peter Deunov became brighter and more radiant. At certain times, I turned around to observe and study further the path I had walked. On this day, I turned around and observed the first elemental realm, with its dominance over the azuric forces, and considered what influence these forces might have on the human being, especially after its complete opening in 2019.

The azuric forces inhabit the human being between the upper luciferic forces and the lower ahrimanic forces, on the lower right side of the Christ forces, which are situated in the area of the heart. There can thus be difficulties in distinguishing the azuric entities from the Christ entity. But in effect they are totally opposite.

Human beings dominated by an azuric entity or force tend to occupy themselves increasingly with murder and death. Then, they can take an interest in killing, either animals or humans. They tend to read about mass murderers or techniques of euthanizing dogs, cats or mink. If they look at pornography, they prefer it to be sadistic, with lots of violence. The occupation with murder and killing can go so far that they really believe that there is an ongoing intention on the part of certain groups to assassinate them, and they recall actual imaginary situations when bullets or knives have been aimed at them – of course, without actually killing them! They also tend fully to believe the most unbelievable theories about secret groups that are supposedly developing methods to kill off a lot of people, either through manipulating weather, adding toxins to fuel or vaccines, or other highly sophisticated methods. They might also be occupied with killing germs, and develop a deep fear for life itself. And they truly and fully believe these visions.

Azuras are DEATH. When I read the lyrics from 'The Future' by Leonard Cohen,* I believe that for a moment he may have experienced the presence of the Azuras. (He may indeed be an old initiate who can travel the elemental realms.) In particular, I would mention these lines: 'Things are going to slide, slide in all directions / Won't be nothing (won't be nothing) / Nothing you can measure anymore.' What does it mean that we can't measure anymore? Number, measure and weight belong to the two elemental realms of atoms and forms, dominated by the ahrimanic and luciferic forces and entities. In the first realm, where the Azuras dominate, there is vacuum, and in this vacuum – where a still unknown but terrible force is hidden – we cannot measure anything. We feel lost there, and this feels like the old order of the spirit is overturned. Indeed, Cohen's is a deep and knowing text...

Then came Sunday (25 July 2021), which, in Vidar's teachings to me, is supposed to be the third day of the sixth cultural age – and, according to the calculations of Rudolf Steiner, around the year 4,000 AD.

The countenance of Peter Deunov was still shining and bright, but a certain change started to appear in his physiognomy. He started to split in two: a male part and a female part. It was like his etheric body – which is always the opposite sex to the physical body – started to part from the physical body and to live an individual life of its own, although in total harmony and connection with the physical body. Between the two human aspects – the male and female – the full moon appeared.

It was like a person with two bodies, parted and united by the moon; not really like in ancient times, when the human being was

---

* 'The Future' by Leonard Cohen: 'Give me back my broken night / My mirrored room, my secret life / It's lonely here / There's no one left to torture / Give me absolute control / Over every living soul / And lie beside me, baby / That's an order / [...] Give me back the Berlin wall / Give me Stalin and St. Paul / I've seen the future, brother / It is murder / Things are going to slide, slide in all directions / Won't be nothing (won't be nothing) / Nothing you can measure anymore / The blizzard, the blizzard of the world / Has crossed the threshold / And it's overturned / The order of the soul / [...]' © Sony/ATV Music Publishing LLC.

androgynous – both male and female in one person – but it was as if the human being was a duality, both male and female, in two persons, and bearing the moon between them. I was amazed, as this coincided with several of Rudolf Steiner's prophesies of the future.

Steiner describes that the etheric body will slowly part from the physical body, making clairvoyance possible – that is, if we have developed sense organs in the etheric body. Further, Steiner spoke of the gradual loss of women's ability to give birth to children. Around the year 6,000, it would vanish completely. When the etheric body, which is the keeper of life forces, separates from the physical body, conceiving a child will of course be very difficult. Then we will have to use the inner or outer etheric in order to help us 'grow' new children, which will be a kind of eugenic occultism (see Appendix 2), which we will be able to master at that time. This eugenic occultism will spring out of, or develop from, the mastering and understanding of the first elemental realm.

Further, Rudolf Steiner said that, around the year 8,000, the moon would reunite with the Earth. The moon will work in the space between the physical body and the etheric body – as they are of the opposite sex – and the moon forces will appear on Earth with the help of the moon beings, as in olden and ancient times. Steiner's words seem clearly to indicate that the physical moon will reunite with the Earth around the year 8,000 AD, although this is very difficult to understand in a literal, scientific sense. If he was indeed describing the moon uniting with the human being between the male and the female, that might be more understandable. Maybe even this uniting could – and I emphasize *could* – really bring the physical moon back to the Earth, although I must say that this seems somewhat far-fetched to me.

During the third day, the moon started to shine more, and it also became more alive. This process lasted until the next day. This 'aliveness' showed itself by the interior of the moon becoming more dynamic, like the interior of an old, handmade watch.

The fourth day – which in this situation is Monday, and also around 4,500-5,000 AD – the image of Peter Deunov became fainter, and likewise its female counterpart, and the workings of the moon became ever more dominant. It started to attract a life of its own, being filled with both *will* and *decision* – not so much feeling and thinking. I wonder what the end result will be…

The same development continued on the fifth day. The moon became more and more dominant – bigger and bigger, and also increasingly stronger. It dominated the whole horizon; it dominated the sky and it also dominated the sun. I felt increasingly uncomfortable with this development.

But then, on the evening of this fifth day, the strength and intensity of the moon started to diminish. The image of Peter Deunov – and at the same time the etheric, female 'double' or 'counterpart' – grew in strength. The strength of the moon, which at a certain point was almost frightening, continued to weaken during the course of the evening.

On the morning of the sixth day, Vidar showed me a moon that was very weak, but again it was in harmony with the other entities or forces: Deunov, the etheric counterpart, and the moon in the middle – all three in a harmonious balance.

Vidar then explained that in ancient times the creative forces of the universe first formed the human being. Then, these forces became conscious and were misused. But humanity learned its lesson and became harmonious again. During the fifth cultural epoch, humanity had to come to harmony with materialism and evil, and during the sixth with the moon forces – which are the growth forces, the creative forces in the etheric body.

Vidar then taught me that – up to the opening of all three elemental realms – most of the seers and initiates of old to a certain extent mistook spiritual development for physical and material development. The three elemental realms are the foundation of the material creation, and when they are closed, the true and deepest secrets of the material world cannot be revealed, even to the higher initiates. The forces in the three elemental realms are also forces and depths that must become conscious, misused and then harmonized, until they are truly understood and integrated.

Vidar then gave me the possibility to imagine that ancient continents like Lemuria and Atlantis might have been spiritual developmental stages and not material and physical phenomena. Likewise, with the future reunion of the moon – and later all the other planets – with the earth. This last teaching caused me to be very quiet and serious. The rest of the sixth day, and also during the seventh, the three entities were in quiet harmony – although Peter Deunov appeared to be the strongest of the three, but not markedly so.

Saturday represented the first day of the seventh cultural age. Now something totally unexpected met me in the morning. It was the appearance of a huge, strong, shining and wise stag, with large antlers that had numerous tines (branches). The stag shone like the sun, and my thoughts were directed to a (Norwegian) book I had bought many years ago called *The Sun Stag*.

During Saturday, Sunday and Monday, the stag stood there quietly, but slowly became more communicative – more and more alive.

On Tuesday, a certain change began to take place – and I say 'began' as I sensed that this would continue further. The stag started to disintegrate into numerous other animals of all kinds. These were quite small, moving all the time – rather like the impression one gets when looking at an ant heap.

This development continued on Wednesday, as the small animals changed appearance into small insects, all fighting each other. Could this represent what Thomas Hobbes referred to as 'the war of all against all'? (This is also hinted at in the thirteenth chapter of St John's 'Book of Revelation'.)

The image of this 'sun stag' that had changed into a heap of crawling, fighting and mindless insects, grew stronger and stronger over the next few days. This picture also became more and more appalling. I had a feeling like sea-sickness – and there were still three days left to go! Besides the development of these images, there was also a kind of 'streaming understanding' of what happened – a kind of love for these developments, and a pity for my fellow humans (including myself, of course) who were to experience this mess, this 'massacre'…

On Friday, something else happened – just as it had on the final days of the foregoing periods. Usually, in the previous periods, it all came to a rest, with nothing dramatic happening. This time, however, something radically changed. The now shrivelling mass of half dead, fighting insects started to transform, and a light began to shine in the darkness around them. It was the light of Christ. After this, the sun stag slowly started to be recreated, and it rose out of the dead insect-mass, like a phoenix – a resurrected Stag of the Sun.

This all happened on the last day of the seventh cultural era (the current period) of the fourth great cycle, the Earth cycle, before the celestial rest, and before the next grand cycle of cultural ages – the beginning of the sixth great cycle, or the second post-Atlantean great cycle or period. Amen.

On the 'resting' day, which was Saturday, everything was quiet. The mass of half dead insects gave the appearance of being 'brewed', whilst the hind part of the stag was still within the mass of insects. Everything was in a process of waiting.

Sunday morning, the first day representing the next great epoch, started with an unexpected vision: an image of a very powerful, red dragon. Together with this vision or image, Vidar gave me a short resume of the evolving Earth, together with its great epochs. He said that it all started in the spiritual realm, a sort of upper Devachan, which we called the Polarian great cycle. Then the next great cycle was experienced in lower Devachan, which we call the Hyperborean age. Then it all condensed during the third great epoch or cycle to the astral plane, which we call the Lemurian phase. Then we experienced everything in the etheric realm, which we call the Atlantean age, when all was etheric and we could stretch our arms in the fluid of the etheric element. That is why this cycle was experienced in water, and if we could 'see' the water structures of old we would 'see' the Atlantean continent. The next great cycle, the fifth, was experienced in the solid or material element, the Earth cycle, which Vidar had described during the previous eight weeks. Now was the time for the sixth great cycle, which he called the 'magical' cycle, or Dragonian epoch, when we are expected to develop magical abilities or powers over the elements, just as the dragons once had, but this time directed by the conscious human mind. This great cycle is intended to be experienced in the elemental kingdoms, in combination with the etheric realm.

The next day, the dragon was still there, but this time some changes or effects took place within my own body. I became – I felt – like a caterpillar, with an outer skin and with strange processes happening within my body, as if my organs had changed and were able to receive additional impulses and inspirations than before.

If indeed this happened to me in order to demonstrate the future changes of the sixth great epoch, which Vidar called the Dragonian great cycle – the great cycle of magic – remains to be seen. I must confess, however, that I felt somewhat changed after this, as if I could see through the Earth itself.

Here I should add a completely personal experience that I had when I was a child. This is described in detail in my book *Experiences from the Threshold*. During my childhood, I could actually see through my father's hands, and this ability lasted for a long time. In fact, I can still do this sometimes today. Now, however, this ability extended to the Earth itself, including the mountains and the elements.

On Tuesday, the following became clear to me: during the seven cultural ages of the first great post-Atlantean cycle, which is the fifth great cycle, all the changes and developments that took place were conceived mentally, within my mind, in concepts and percepts. Now, in the sixth great cycle, the teachings and developments were felt as bodily changes, as real changes within my organs, brain and body. The first change was in the brain. The next change was felt just below my diaphragm, in the stomach. I now consider that such organic changes are necessary for the development of the human species – as it seemed that the mental development was not sufficient to change our course from destruction. We have to change the sense organs – the organs themselves – in order to be able to save humanity; in order to develop the three occultisms and to be able to change the dying world into the next planetary stage, the Jupiter incarnation.

Now, in order for me better to understand such changes, I wonder if this teaching simply indicates the coming bodily changes, or if some of these changes will also affect my own body? I will try and monitor changes in my life and work.

The next area to experience a change was in my throat and neck. I experienced a strange activity there during the next day, but I could not trace any differences in my thinking, feeling or will during my work on the Wednesday. (This activity in my throat continued for some time – now more directly within the throat itself.)

Then, the next day, on Friday, the development moved to my heart, a little below and behind. (That reminded me of what the 'hidden people' in Iceland had told me some years ago, that the new heart organ would be precisely in that region.) I now realized that this development was about developing organs for thinking, feeling and will – for more spiritual organs than we had until now – that would enable us to use the powers of these three soul forces truly to work into the world through the powers of this new age, the magical age when we would be able to change the material world through a kind of magic or occultism steered and initiated through our own thinking, feeling and will.

The eighth day, Saturday, was quiet. Sunday is expected to be a day of rest, and then Monday would follow. But, although

Sunday was a resting day, the teaching went on nevertheless, although nothing substantial actually happened or developed on this day. I was shown the 'new' human being, ready for the magical age, when humanity's goal is to transform the earth totally – to spiritualize the material creation into a spiritual state of divinity and good.

This new human being stood there in front of my spiritual eyes, strong and healthy, full of good will, with a Christ-imbued countenance, receiving the forces of both the cosmos in its twelve-fold diversity and also the two-fold etheric, as well as the forces of the Earth: the three-fold elemental world in its four-fold, its ten-fold and its seventeen-fold strength and complexity.

Monday, which I thought would be the first day of the second cultural period, was totally quiet. So it seems that the length of the cultural periods in the sixth great cycle were longer than in the fifth great cycle. It seems to have been a minor shift in the rhythm. At that stage, I lost track of the years in which this would all unfold, but I believe it would be around the year 11,000 AD.

Tuesday came with a continuation of the teachings, and I was shown, partly as an image and partly as an experience within myself – as when Vidar demonstrated the reorganizing of my organs – how the new thinking would be able to change the world.

At 4.12 am I woke up with a command from Vidar, to go down into the living room and look at a certain page in the book on 'Seth' that I had ordered previously and that had arrived the day before. I did, and found to my surprise that the whole page was specifically about how a strengthened thinking could change both the past and the future.

After this, my understanding of the time-line in the teachings became somewhat uncertain. The further I was able to enter the future, the faster time passed. In the beginning of the teachings, concerning our own great period, each of the cultural ages lasted seven days, with a following day of rest. Now time speeded up. In the beginning I thought that each cultural age was one day, with one resting day in between – but now this also speeded up. Increasingly, too, I experienced the teachings internally, and less as imaginations as such. In other words, I experienced changes inside my own body.

Inside my head, mirrors were splintered. I experienced evil in the world inside myself, and my body was transformed, as described by Anne Catherine Emmerich. (She helped people by taking their diseases into herself, struggling with the karma and the disease for two or three days, and then becoming well again, although somewhat weakened through the process.)

One night, I woke up and a mosquito was sucking my blood. I took the creature into my soul, experiencing the material prison it was in. Usually, we meet evil – ahrimanic, luciferic and azuric entities – and push them away. I learned that they must be taken into ourselves with love, and transformed in the name of the Christ, with Christ consciousness.

When I stood up the next morning I received the deep realization that we have to do this with all evil, even with vaccines. I could in fact let myself be vaccinated and take the azuric beings contained within the vaccine – or the poisons, if you like – and transform them in the light of the Christ, through the heart and the love of the *Sacre Coeur* (sacred heart of Jesus), and let this transformed evil radiate out into the world.

The very next day, I gave a course in France, close to Cerne. We travelled to Cerne with a group of therapists in order to see if we could transform some of the darkness radiating out from there – a dark evil of azuric origin. What we did that day was amazing. We transformed the azuric energy in Cerne, and we did the same with a 5G mast there. We let the Christ force into the so-called Hartman and Curry lines of the Earth.*

---

* The terrestrial magnetic field is formed by grids known as global networks. These are preferred channels of energy circulation. Above these grids, low intensity radiation of natural origin is concentrated, often imperceptible to most people. The most well-known global network was discovered in the mid-twentieth century by Dr Ernst Hartmann. It is described in detail in his book *Krankheit als Standortproblem* ('The disease as a localization problem'). The doctor deduced its existence by comparing thousands of georhythmographs. His work indicated that the electrical resistance of the human body was decomposed on a grid oriented by the cardinal points and that acquired his name. In mid-latitudes, they are parallel lines with a distance of 2.5m East-West and 2m North-South. Between these geometric lines there is a neutral zone. The intensity of the Hartmann lines increases during the night. Therefore, the effects on human health occur especially during the hours of sleep. Dr Hartmann provides evidence of effects on human health in his book. They occur especially in the points located above the vertical of a Hartmann network crossing or a single Hartmann line crossing with other geological disturbances such as groundwater or faults, usually in the form of an increase in anxiety, insomnia, trembling and cramps.

The following day, much had changed. A dowser would detect that all negativity in the Hartmann and Curry lines, to a radius of seven kilometers, was totally gone. The darkness over Cerne was lighter, and the lake of Geneva was brighter. The most interesting aspect of this work was the observation that a changed or transformed evil elemental being now radiated its new Christ-content, so that the healing effect spread out. I have also seen this with the Covid-19 vaccines.

Later in the week, time sped up too fast to make any firm reference, although the main teaching I was given was that everything of the Earth was to be internalized and Christianized. Time was like a parable – it went faster and faster as we advanced into the future. Then the period of Earth was over. The teachings had reached their end, and I was ready to enter spirit land itself, which I now did.

*

At this point, my intention was to end this book, and to leave the rest for my next book, which was intended to be about spirit land. Then something changed my decision. I walked the spirit land for several days, until a friend from England asked me to ask Vidar a specific – and for my friend an important – question. This question was about the future incarnation of Ahriman.

This needs some explanation, as well as the answer itself. As we saw previously (see p. 4), Rudolf Steiner predicted that Ahriman would incarnate in the flesh in the first part of the third millennium, which is the beginning of the millennium in which we are now living. How, when and in whom this incarnation would take place, has been a much-discussed question among anthroposophists for many years. Steiner described this incarnation several times.* Some of the main characteristics of this incarnated Ahriman would be extreme intelligence – he himself would be a master – and that he would start a mystery school where everybody could learn to become clairvoyant. However, this clairvoyance would be of a false nature, so that everybody would ultimately disagree on spiritual matters. As a consequence, Ahriman would win.

Vidar's answer was clear and simple, and as I slowly pondered this it made more and more sense. He said that Ahriman was already in the process of incarnating, at this very time, but that he is

---

* See Rudolf Steiner, *The Incarnation of Ahriman* (Rudolf Steiner Press 2006).

incarnating in all of us, with the help – or by being given cover by – the azuric beings. *It is extremely important to understand this.*

As mentioned previously in this book, for some time I had observed that a third force, a third type of entity, has been incarnating in the human body. These entities are azuric, and lingering in the first realm of the elemental world, which opened to human access around the year 2019. I have also observed that these beings were able to give the 'carrier' (of the entity) some degree of clairvoyance, but that this clairvoyance was always false. Usually, the adversarial entities give information that was ninety per cent true and ten per cent false. This make the carrier believe in themselves, and thus to continue to connect with the adversarial beings and forces for eternity.

In fact, I had observed that this azuric-initiated clairvoyance dominated around eighty per cent of all those that claimed such abilities (those who had a life-income from them, gave courses and/or wrote books). I had spoken to a few such persons. Whilst some admitted that this was the case and tried to change their ways, many denied it was true, as they feared they would lose their reputation and income.

I had not understood why these azuric beings could provide such clairvoyance, but now, after pondering Vidar's answer, I understood perfectly.

Ahriman is in the process of incarnating NOW. Ahriman is incarnating in ALL people – also myself – and especially spiritual people, with the help of the azuric elementals. In this way, he incarnates, hides himself and also initiates a 'school' of magic, leading to clairvoyance – a clairvoyance that is personal and that nobody can agree on.

This answer to the question was so important that I had to add it to this book at the very last moment before it went into print.

Are Thoresen, October 2021

Appendix 1

The Northern Path in History

This book is based on my own experiences practicing the Nordic path of initiation, the Nordic tradition that I belong to, as well as Rudolf Steiner's anthroposophy. Thus, in general I speak of the threshold, the three elemental realms and the etheric world beyond – both the 'inner' etheric world as well as the 'outer' etheric world – in a Nordic and European context, as well as, of course, in anthroposophic concepts. In this Appendix, I will consider some of the historical sources and associations connected to this path, as I understand it.

From the Våluspå:*

61. She sees arising
Once again
Earth from the waters,
Green once more.
The floods abate,
The erne flies over,
Who from the fells
Goes down to fish.

62. The Æsir meet
On Ida field,
Hold counsel of
The great earth thong.
There they recall

---

* Old Norse, 'Prophecy of the Seeress', is the first and best-known poem of the *Poetic Edda*. It tells the story of the creation of the world and its coming end. It is one of the most important primary sources for the study of Norse mythology. Henry Adam Bellows proposed a tenth-century dating and authorship by a pagan Icelander with knowledge of Christianity. He also assumes the early hearers would have been very familiar with the 'story' of the poem and not in need of an explanation.

Great words of old,
And the far runes
Of Fimbultyr.

63. Thereafter again
Shall be found on the grass
The wondrous golden balls
That in old days they owned.

64. The fields unsown
Again will grow;
Bad shall be better,
Balder return;
Höður and Balder shall dwell
In the Father's Heaven,
Truly the gods of the slain.
Know ye of that, or what?

65. Then can Hönir
Choose his lot,
[…]
And sons of two brothers
Shall dwell in Windheim.
Know ye of that, or what?

66. A Hall she sees standing,
More bright than the sun,
Thatched all with gold,
On Gimil's height.
Then shall the true folk dwell
Ever in joy.

67. Then comes the ruling of the Mighty Doom
In power from above,
Which speaks to all.

68. Now the dark dragon
Comes flying, the adder
Down from the Niðafells.

He bears on his wings,
Flying over the plain,
The dead serpent of Hate.
Now she sinks; can no more.[*]

Commentary:

The narrative describes the death or loss of the old world, dominated by the old gods, and the resurrection or birth of a new one. Here, Vidar dominates, although this is not clearly defined (because Vidar is both the godly opponent of the ahrimanic adversarial forces in the second realm of the elemental world, as well as the guardian of the threshold of the outer etheric world, and also the presenter or 'face' of Christ in this outer etheric world).

The 'old' etheric world, where the old gods have their reign, is described as the 'inner' etheric world, with all its forces of nature. Then we go through the three realms of the elemental world, where there is a fight between the three groups of adversarial powers and the gods. In this fight, the dominion of the old gods fades and, in coming through the elemental world, we enter the 'outer' etheric world. Here Vidar and Balder stand as guardians of the threshold. In this world, which feels new when arriving there for the first time, we may find the Christ.

From the Kalevala:[†]

Marjatta, child of beauty,
Magic maid of little stature,
Guarded well her sacred virtue,
Her sincerity and honour,
Fed upon the dainty whiting,
On the inner bark of birch-wood,
On the tender flesh of lambkins.
[...]

---

[*] Source: http://www.germanicmythology.com/PoeticEdda/

[†] A nineteenth-century work of epic poetry, regarded as the national epic of Karelia and Finland and one of the most significant works of Finnish literature.

It was but the mountain-berry
Calling to the lonely maiden:
'Come, O virgin, come and pluck me,
Come and take me to thy bosom,
Take me, tinsel-breasted virgin,
Take me, maiden, copper-belted,
Ere the slimy snail devours me,
Ere the black-worm feeds upon me.
Hundreds pass my way unmindful,
Thousands come within my hearing,
Berry-maidens swarm about me,
Marjatta, child of beauty,
Listened to its gentle pleading,
Ran to pick the berry, calling,
With her fair and dainty fingers.
Saw it smiling near the meadow,
Like a cranberry in feature,
Like a strawberry in flavour;
But be Virgin, Marjatta,
Could not pluck the woodland-stranger,
Thereupon she cut a charm-stick,
Downward pressed upon the berry,
When it rose as if by magic,
Rose above her shoes of ermine,
Then above her copper girdle,
Darted upward to her bosom,
Leaped upon the maiden's shoulder,
On her dimpled chin it rested,
On her lips it perched a moment,
Hastened to her tongue expectant
To and fro it rocked and lingered,
Thence it hastened on its journey,
Settled in the maiden's bosom.
Marjatta, child of beauty,
Thus became a bride impregnate,
Wedded to the mountain-berry;
Lingered in her room at morning,
Sat at midday in the darkness,
Hastened to her couch at evening.

Thus the watchful mother wonders:
'What has happened to our Mary,
To our virgin, Marjatta'.*

Commentary:
That Rudolf Steiner chose Finland as the place where he gave his
description of the Northern path does not come as a surprise when
we read these lines from the *Kalevala* – a magical poem that refers
directly to the structure and order of the spiritual world, and also to
the Nordic stream of initiation. We hear that Marjatta is out in the forest, walking in snow, and then starts to 'fade' into a red berry – a ling-
onberry. Through these means, she crosses the threshold, and the rest
of the song is about what she experiences there – but note that she
meets three obstacles, three guardians of the threshold, transposed
into the material world.

From Parsifal:†

Arthur has ridden from his castle at Karidoel in search of the Red
Knight (Parzival), who has spared him from Ither. He wants to
make him one of his knights. It is a snowy May day. Parzival, on a
field at Joflanze, next to the Plimizoel river, sees blood drops in the
pure white snow (from a goose attacked by Arthur's falcon), and is
reminded of his beloved Condwiramurs. He stares at the red blood-
drops in the white snow, and 'fades' or 'merges' deep into them. He
is somewhat lost to the world, and neither hears anything nor sees
anything else than the red in the white snow. While he sits like this,
he raises his lance, unknowingly, not thinking about this as a sign of
battle. As such, Parzival gives a signal to the world that he is ready
to fight. Sitting thus, totally emerged in the spiritual world, having passed the threshold to the elemental world, three opponents
appear (the three adversarial forces). A squire from Cunneware
encounters him and cries out. The reckless Segramors comes and
wants to fight Parzival. He rides against him with his lance raised,

---

* Source: https://www.sacred-texts.com/neu/kveng/kvrune50.htm

† An epic poem, one of the masterpieces of the Middle Ages, written between
1200 and 1210 in Middle High German by Wolfram von Eschenbach.

but just before he hits him Parzival 'wakes up' and takes him down. Segramors attacks, but loses. Parzival goes back into his meditative state, and is still lost in thoughts of love. The author apostrophizes Lady Love (Minne). Subsequently, Keie challenges him but also loses the fight. The author alludes to his patron Herman, the Landgrave of Thuringia, and to the poet and Minnesinger Walther von der Vogelweide, and praises Keie. Gawan* rides out, covers up the drops of blood to allow Parzival to recover his wits, and escorts Parzival to Arthur's camp, telling him of Gawan's father, Lot. Parzival is the Waleis, 'the flower of all men', still beardless and radiant with beauty. Cunneware welcomes him, appreciating that Parzival has avenged the wrong that Keie did to her. Parzival is cleaned up and dressed, meets Arthur, and is made a knight of the Round Table. Guinevere joins them, and forgives Parzival for killing Ither. Then Parzival travels onwards and in the end finds his way back to the Grail castle. But without this central experience, his journey would have been impossible.[†]

Commentary:
The whole story of *Parzival* is closely related or linked to the Northern stream of initiation, and parallels closely the narrative of *Våluspå*. First, Parzival wanders the external world, makes his mistakes but still knows that he is in search of the spiritual life. Then, on a May day, in the snow, he sees the red blood drops and fades or merges into them. By fading into this red colour of nature, he enters the elemental realm of existence, and immediately three men on horses appear in the form of three knights (the three realms of the elemental world), challenging him, as he is sitting on his horse with his lance in the air – a certain sign in those days that you were challenging to fight. He wins over all three opponents. Then the way to the Grail castle is reopened (the outer etheric world), and he can continue his search for the Grail (finding Christ in the outer etheric world).

---

* Gawan comes from Norway, son of King Lot and Sangive, and thus fits very well into this description of the Northern stream of initiation.

[†] I am grateful to Michael McGoodwin for this summary (www.mcgoodwin. net), on which this text is based.

Rudolf Steiner's School of Spiritual Science, the First Class:*

If we pass the threshold according to the Southern way of initiation, according to all esoteric teachings including Rudolf Steiner's, we meet three fierce animals at the threshold. These three animals are – they do not *represent*, they *are* in reality – the mistaken, inverted or misinterpreted thinking, feeling and will that we have developed over time, and that stand in the way of a real spiritual conception of the spiritual world. The 'animals of the threshold' are creatures or projections of our own undeveloped thinking, feeling and will. They are there to remind us that when we separate these soul-faculties, we will see them as they are, full of faults, mistakes, lies and weaknesses. If we don't recognize these faults before we pass the threshold, the adversaries will use them in their own play of power, and we will be lost to their forces. It seems to me that these three animals are also our illusions in and of the three realms of the elemental world, as well as in thinking, feeling and will.

Rudolf Steiner's Philosophy of Freedom:†

There are correspondences between the Northern way of entering the spiritual world, outlined in this book, and the path outlined by

---

* Rudolf Steiner outlines the task of the First Class of the School of Spiritual Science as follows. 'In general ... it will be necessary for human beings to get to know the spiritual world first in the form of ideas. This is how spiritual science is cultivated in the General Anthroposophical Society. However, there will be people who want to participate in portrayals of the spiritual world that progress upwards from the form of ideas to manners of expression that are borrowed from the spiritual world itself. There will also be people who want to get to know the paths to the spiritual world in order to tread them with their own souls. The three Classes of the School will be for them.' (*Die Konstitution der Allgemeinen Anthroposophischen Gesellschaft und der freien Hochschule für Geisteswissenschaft*, Rudolf Steiner Verlag 1987, GA 260a, p.108f.)

† *The Philosophy of Freedom* is Rudolf Steiner's fundamental philosophical work. It addresses the question of whether and in what sense human beings can be said to be free. Originally published in 1894 in German as *Die Philosophie der Freiheit*, with a second edition published in 1918, the work has appeared under a number of English titles, including *The Philosophy of Spiritual Activity* (the title Steiner proposed for the English-language translation), *The Philosophy of Freedom* (Rudolf Steiner Press 2011), and *Intuitive Thinking as a Spiritual Path* (SteinerBooks 1995).

Rudolf Steiner in his early book *The Philosophy of Freedom*. In his lecture cycle *The Boundaries of Natural Science* (from 1920), Steiner speaks about two anthroposophical paths: the meditative path connected to his book *Knowledge of the Higher Worlds* (designated as more traditional and connected to the East), and *The Philosophy of Freedom* (designated as more contemporary and ideal for the West).

It appears that the more modern path has several important similarities to the Northern way, some of which are as follows. Moral actions in *The Philosophy of Freedom* are attained purely out of one's own uniting with forces of love and freedom. In a similar manner, the moral world is described in the Northern way as being bestowed through piercing the sense world. In both cases there is an absence of the requirement for obedience to a prescribed external moral code, and also the absence of a guardian with an objective moral determination. Similarly, *The Philosophy of Freedom* provides a training in the separation of aspects of one's cognition and soul forces, to rise to new levels of awareness, for instance, in becoming aware of the division of reality into percept and concept, and also the different types of thinking activity. This conscious splitting of selective sense and/or soul forces also appears as a necessary aspect of the Northern way of initiation, as outlined here.

In the lectures mentioned above, Steiner is clear that the role of *The Philosophy of Freedom* is to strengthen the thinking sufficiently in order to allow concept-free access to the sense world ('merging'). After attaining pure thinking (in which the ego can live and maintain a firm footing), then *'this thinking can then be excluded from the process of perception'*. Whereas in ordinary life one sees colour, let us say, and at the same time imbues the colour with conceptual activity, one can now extract the concepts from the entire process of elaborating percepts, and draw the percept itself directly into one's bodily constitution. Steiner says:

> Sense perception, together with its content, passes down into the organism, and the ego with its pure thought content remains, so to speak, hovering above. We exclude thinking inasmuch as we take into and fill ourselves with the whole content of the perception, instead of weakening it with concepts, as we usually do.*

---

* *The Boundaries of Natural Science*, Lecture 7, SteinerBooks 1987.

It is possible to pursue this path in a way consonant with Western life if we attempt to surrender ourselves completely to the world of outer phenomena, so that we allow them to work upon us without thinking about them but still perceiving them. In ordinary waking life, you will agree, we are constantly perceiving, but actually in the very process of doing so we are continually saturating our percepts with concepts; in scientific thinking we interweave percepts and concepts entirely systematically, building up systems of concepts and so on. By having acquired the capacity for the kind of thinking that gradually emerges from *The Philosophy of Freedom*, one can become capable of such acute inner activity that one can exclude and suppress conceptual thinking from the process of perception and surrender oneself to bare percepts.[*]

And, pure thinking is related to exhalation just as perception is related to inhalation.[†]

From Rudolf Steiner's lecture in Helsinki on 3 April 1912:[‡]

First of all, looking away from the earth, if we direct our gaze into the ranges of cosmic space, we are met by the blue sky. Suppose we do this on a day in which no cloud, not even the faintest silver-white cloudlet breaks the azure space of heaven. We look upwards into this blue heaven spread out above us — whether we recognize it in the physical sense as something real or not, does not signify; the point is the impression that this wide stretch of the blue heavens makes upon us. Suppose that we can yield ourselves up to this blue of the sky, and that we do this with intensity and for a long, long time; that we can do it so

---

[*] Ibid.

[†] Ibid., Lecture 8.

[‡] From Rudolf Steiner, *The Spiritual Beings in the Heavenly Bodies and in the Kingdoms of Nature*, Lecture 1, op.cit.

that we forget all else that we know in life and all that is around us in life. Suppose that we are able for one moment to forget all the external impressions, all our memories, all the cares and troubles of life, and can yield ourselves completely to the single impression of the blue heavens. What I am now saying to you can be experienced by every human soul if only it will fulfil these necessary conditions; what I am telling you can be a common human experience. Suppose a human soul gazes in this way at nothing but the blue of the sky. A certain moment then comes, a moment in which the blue sky ceases to be blue — in which we no longer see anything which can in human language be called blue. If at that moment when the blue to us ceases to be blue, we turn our attention to our own soul, we shall notice quite a special mood in it. The blue disappears, and as it were, an infinity arises before us, and in this infinity a quite definite mood in our soul; a quite definite feeling, a quite definite perception pours itself into the emptiness which arises where the blue had been before. If we would give a name to this soul perception, to that which would soar out there into infinite distances, there is only one word for it; it is a devout feeling in our soul, a feeling of pious devotion to infinity. All the religious feelings in the evolution of humanity have fundamentally a nuance which contains within it what I have here called a pious devotion; the impression of the blue vault of the heavens which stretches above us has called up a religious feeling, a moral perception. When within our souls the blue has disappeared, a moral perception of the external world springs to life.

Let us now reflect upon another feeling by means of which we can in another way attune ourselves in moral harmony with external nature. When the trees are bursting into leaf and the meadows are filled with green, let us fix our gaze upon the green which in the most varied manner covers the earth or meets us in the trees; and again we will do this in such a way as to forget all the external impressions which can affect our souls, and simply devote ourselves to that which in external nature meets us as green. If once more we are so circumstanced that we can yield ourselves to that which springs forth as the reality of green, we can carry this so far that the green disappears for us, in the same way as previously the blue as blue disappeared. Here again we cannot say, 'a colour is spread out before our sight', but (and I remark expressly that I am telling you of things that everyone can experience for himself if he fulfils the requisite conditions) the soul has instead a peculiar feeling, which can be thus expressed: 'I now understand what I experience when I think creatively, when a thought springs up in me, when an idea strikes me: I understand this now for the first time, I can only learn this from the bursting forth of the green all around me. I begin to understand the inmost parts of my soul through external nature when the outer natural impression has disappeared and, in its place, a moral impression is left. The green of the plant tells me how I ought to feel within myself, when my soul is blessed with the power to think thoughts, to cherish ideas.' Here again an external impression of nature is transmuted into a moral feeling.

Or again we may look at a wide stretch of white snow. In the same way as in the description just given of the blue of the sky and the green of earth's robe of vegetation, so this too can set free within us a moral feeling for all that we call the phenomenon of matter in the world. And if, in contemplation of the white snow mantle, we can forget everything else, and experience the whiteness, and then allow it to disappear, we obtain an understanding of that which fills the earth as substance, as matter. We then feel matter living and weaving in the world. And just as one can transform all external sight-impressions into moral perceptions, so too can one transform impressions of sound into moral perceptions. Suppose we listen to a tone and then to its octave, and so attune our souls to this dual sound of a tonic note and its octave that we forget all the rest, eliminate all the rest and completely yield ourselves to these tones, it comes about at last that, instead of hearing these dual tones, our attention is directed from these and we no longer hear them. Then again, we find that in our soul a moral feeling is set free. We begin then to have a spiritual understanding of what we experience when a wish lives within us that tries to lead us to something, and then our reason influences our wish. The concord of wish and reason, of thought and desire, as they live in the human soul, is perceived in the tone and its octave.

Commentary:
In my experience, this description is very much parallel to what I describe as my way into these realms. Even the presence of the guardian of the threshold is omitted, as it is only present when one passes the elemental realms. In entering the 'inner' etheric world, the guardian is not found; in passing the three elemental realms he is only found in the physical world; and in entering the 'outer' etheric world, the guardian is finally met in the shape of Vidar and Balder.

We should also bear in mind that during the one hundred or so years since Rudolf Steiner held these lectures, as well as the nineteen lessons of the First Class, much has changed in the spiritual world, the thresholds and the adversarial forces and entities.

Appendix 2

Rudolf Steiner on the Three 'Occultisms'

On 1 December 1918,* Rudolf Steiner spoke about mechanistic, eugenic and hygienic occultism as follows:

> This threefold capacity, of which every knowing person within these secret circles speaks — these three capacities that will evolve in human nature, I must make intelligible to you in the following way. First, there are the capacities having to do with so-called material occultism. By means of this capacity — and this is precisely the ideal of British secret societies — certain social forms at present basic within the industrial system shall be set up on an entirely different foundation. Every knowing member of these secret circles is aware that, solely by means of certain capacities that are still latent but evolving in man, and with the help of the law of harmonious oscillations, machines and mechanical constructions and other things can be set in motion. A small indication is to be found in what I connected with the person of Strader in my Mystery Dramas.
>
> These things are at present in process of development. They are guarded as secrets within those secret circles in the field of material occultism. Motors can be set in motion, into activity, by an insignificant human influence through a knowledge of the corresponding curve of oscillation. By means of this principle it will be possible to substitute merely mechanical forces for human forces in many things. The number of human beings on the earth today in actual fact is 1,400,000,000. Labour is performed however, not only by these 1,400,000,000 persons — as I once explained here — but so much labour is performed in a merely mechanical way that we say the earth is really inhabited by 2,000,000,000 persons. The others are simply machines. That is, if the work that is done by machines

---

* See *The Challenge of the Times* (GA 186), Anthroposophic Press 1979.

had to be done by people without machines, it would be necessary to have 600,000,000 more persons on the earth. If what I am now discussing with you under the name of mechanistic occultism enters into the field of practical action, which is the ideal of those secret centres, it will be possible to accomplish the work not only of 500,000,000 or 600,000,000 but of 1,080,000,000 persons. The possibility will thus come about of rendering unnecessary nine-tenths of the work of individuals within the regions of the English-speaking peoples. Mechanistic occultism will not only render it possible to do without nine-tenths of the labour still performed at present by human hands, but will give the possibility also of paralyzing every uprising attempted by the then dissatisfied masses of humanity.

The capacity to set motors in motion according to the laws of reciprocal oscillations will develop on a great scale among the English-speaking peoples. This is known in their secret circles, and is counted upon as the means whereby the mastery over the rest of the population of the earth shall be achieved even in the course of the fifth post-Atlantean epoch. [By revealing this, Steiner undermined its power and potential – AT.] Something else is known also in those circles. It is known that there are two other capacities that will likewise develop. One, which I shall venture to call the eugenic capacity, will evolve primarily among people of the East, of Russia and the Asiatic hinterland. It is also known in those secret circles of the West that this eugenic occultism will not evolve out of the inborn potentialities of the English-speaking peoples, but only of the inborn potentialities belonging precisely to the Asiatic and the Russian populations. These facts are known in the secret circles of the West. They are taken into account and are looked upon as constituting certain motive forces that must become active in future evolution.

By the eugenic capacity I mean the removal of the reproduction of human beings from the sphere of mere arbitrary impulse and accident. Among the peoples of the East there will gradually develop a brilliantly clear knowledge as to how the laws of population, the laws of peopling the earth, must run parallel with certain cosmic phenomena. From this information they will know that, if conception is brought about in accord with certain constellations of the stars, opportunities will thus be given for souls that are either good or evil in their natures to obtain access for earthly incarnation. This capacity will be acquired only by those individuals who constitute the continuation as races, the continuation in the blood stream, of the Asiatic population. They will be able simply to see in detail how what works today chaotically and arbitrarily in conception and birth can be brought into harmony with the great laws of the cosmos in individual concrete cases. Here abstract laws are of no avail. What will be acquired is a concrete single capacity in which it will be known in individual cases whether or not a conception should occur at a particular time.

This knowledge, which will make it possible to bring down from the heavens the impelling forces for the moralizing or demoralizing of the earth through the nature of man himself, this special capacity evolves as a continuation of the blood capacity in the races of the East. What evolves as a capacity, there I call eugenic occultism. This is the second capacity — the capacity that will prevent the evolution of humanity as regards conception and birth from taking its course according to arbitrary impulses, and more or less accidentally. I beg you to consider the enormous social consequences, the enormous social motive forces that enter here! These capacities are latent. It is well known in those secret circles of the English-speaking peoples that these capacities will evolve among the peoples of the East. They know that they themselves will not possess these capacities within their own potentialities bestowed upon them through birth. They know that the earth could not reach its goal, could not pass over from earth to Jupiter — indeed, they know that the earth would within a relatively short time diverge from the path leading to its goal if only the forces belonging to the West should be employed. It would gradually come about that only a soulless population could evolve in the West, a population that would be as soulless as possible. This is known. For this reason, these people endeavour to develop within their own circles, through their capacities, mechanistic occultism. The endeavour is also made to establish a mastery over those peoples who will develop eugenic occultism. Every instructed person in the circles of the West says, for example, 'It is necessary that we rule over India for the reason that only through the continuation of what comes out of Indian bodies — when this unites with what tends in the West in a wholly different direction, in the direction of mechanistic occultism — can bodies come into existence in which souls will be able to incarnate in future who will carry the earth over to its future evolutionary stages.' The English-speaking occultists know that they cannot depend upon the bodies that come out of the fundamental character of their own people, and so they strive to possess the mastery over a people who will provide bodies with the help of which the evolution of the earth may be carried forward in the future.

The American occultists know that they can never carry over into the future what they will to carry over unless they nurture what will develop in the form of bodies for the future within the Russian population through its eugenic occult potentialities, unless they gain the mastery of this, so that a social union can gradually come into existence between their own decadent race characteristics and the germinating psychic race characteristics of European Russia.

I must speak to you also regarding a third capacity, which is latent today but which will evolve. This is what I venture to call the hygienic occult capacity. Now we have all three: the materialistic occult capacity, the eugenic occult capacity, and the hygienic occult capacity. This hygienic occult capacity is well on its way and will not be long, relatively speaking, in arriving. This capacity will come to maturity simply through the insight that human life, in its course from birth to death, progresses in a manner identical with the process of an illness. Processes of illnesses are, in other words, only special and radical transmutations of the quite ordinary, normal life process taking its course between birth and death, except that we bear within ourselves not only the forces that create illness but also those that heal. These healing forces, as every occultist knows, are precisely the same as those that are applied when a person acquires occult capacities, in which case these forces are transmuted into the forces of knowledge. The healing power innate in the human organism, when transmuted into knowledge, gives occult forms of knowledge.

Now, every knowing person in the Western circles is aware that materialistic medicine will have no basis in the future. As soon as the hygienic occult capacities evolve, a person will need no external material medicine, but the possibility will exist of treating prophylactically in a psychic way to prevent those illnesses that do not arise through karmic causes because karmic illnesses cannot be influenced. Everything in this respect will change. This seems at present like a mere fantasy, but it is actually something that will soon come about. Now, the situation is such that these three faculties will not come into existence equally among all the peoples of the earth. Indeed, you have already seen the differentiation. This differentiation has to do, naturally, only with the bodies and not with the souls, which always pass, of course, from race to race, from people to people. But with the bodies this differentiation has much to do. From the bodies of the English-speaking peoples the possibility of developing eugenic occult capacities in the future through birth can never arise. It is precisely in the West that these will be applied, but the manner in which they will be applied will be that a mastery will be established over the Eastern lands, and marriages will be brought about between people of the West and people of the East. Thus use will be made of what can be learned only from the people of the East.

The potentiality of hygienic occult capacities is present in special measure among the people of the Central countries. English-speaking people cannot acquire the hygienic occult capacities through their inborn potentialities, but they can acquire these capacities in their development in the course of time between birth and death. These can become acquired characteristics during that time. In the case of the population occupying the area approximately eastward from the Rhine and all the way into Asia, these capacities will be present on the basis of birth. The population of the Central countries cannot acquire the eugenic occult potentialities through birth, but may acquire them in the course of their lives if they become apprentices of the people of the East. It is in this way that these capacities will be distributed. The people of the East will have not the least capacity for material occultism; they will be able to receive this only when it is given to them, when it is not kept secret from them. It will always be possible to keep it secret, especially when the others are so stupid as not to believe in things that are asserted by a person who is in a position to see into them. In other words the people of the East and those of the Central countries will have to receive material occultism from the West. They will receive its benefits, its products. Hygienic occultism will develop primarily in the Central countries, and eugenic occultism in the Eastern lands. It will be necessary, however, for intercommunication to exist between people. This is something that must be taken up into the impelling forces of the social order of the future. It makes it imperative for people to see that they will be able to live in future throughout the world only as total human beings. If an American should wish to live only as an American, although he would be able to achieve the loftiest material results, he would condemn himself to the fate of never progressing beyond earthly evolution. If he should not seek social relationships with the East, he would condemn himself to being bound within the earthly sphere after a certain incarnation, haunting the sphere of the earth like a ghost. The earth would be drawn away from its cosmic connections, and all these souls would have to be like ghosts. Correspondingly, if the people of the East should not take up the materialism of the West with their eugenic occult capacities that pull down the earth, the Eastern man would lose the earth. He would be drawn into some sort of mere psychic-spiritual evolution, and he would lose the earthly evolution. The earth would sink away under him as it were, and he would not be able to possess the fruit of the earthly evolution.

Mutual confidence among people in a profound inner sense is what must come about. This is manifest through their remarkable future evolution.

A note from the publisher

For more than a quarter of a century, **Temple Lodge Publishing** has made available new thought, ideas and research in the field of spiritual science.

Anthroposophy, as founded by Rudolf Steiner (1861-1925), is commonly known today through its practical applications, principally in education (Steiner-Waldorf schools) and agriculture (biodynamic food and wine). But behind this outer activity stands the core discipline of spiritual science, which continues to be developed and updated. True science can never be static and anthroposophy is living knowledge.

Our list features some of the best contemporary spiritual-scientific work available today, as well as introductory titles. So, visit us online at **www.templelodge.com** and join our emailing list for news on new titles.

If you feel like supporting our work, you can do so by buying our books or making a direct donation (we are a non-profit/charitable organisation).

office@templelodge.com

For the finest books of Science and Spirit